Film as Social Practice

Studies in Culture and Communication
General Editor: John Fiske

Film as Social Practice

Second edition

Graeme Turner

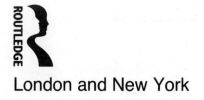

London and New York

First published in 1988
by Routledge

Reprinted 1990, 1991, 1992

This edition published in 1993
by Routledge
11 New Fetter Lane, London EC4P 4EE

Simultaneously published in the USA and Canada
by Routledge
29 West 35th Street, New York, NY 10001

© 1988, 1993 Graeme Turner

Typeset in 10/12pt Times by Florencetype Ltd, Kewstoke, Avon
Printed and bound in Great Britain by Clays, St Ives plc

British Library Cataloguing in Publication Data
A catalogue record for this book is available from the British Library

Library of Congress Cataloging in Publication Data
Turner, Graeme.
    Film as social practice / Graeme Turner. – 2nd ed.
        p. cm.—(Studies in culture and communication)
    Includes bibliographical references and index.
    1. Motion pictures—Social aspects. 2. Communication. I/ Title.
II. Series.
PN1995.9.S6T87 1993
302.2'343—dc20
93-12787
ISBN 0-415-092728

This is for Jessie
who missed out last time

Contents

List of illustrations

Acknowledgements

For assistance with, and permission to reproduce, the illustrations in this book I would like to thank: John Fairfax and Sons; A.A.P.; Time-Life; Fox/Columbia (Australia); Village Roadshow; Philip Neilsen; Meg Labrum; the National Film and Sound Archive of Australia; Kakanda Pty Ltd; the *Border Morning Mail* (Albury); Twentieth Century Fox; and Associated R & R Films.

General editor's preface

This series of books on different aspects of communication is designed to meet the needs of the growing number of students coming to study this subject for the first time. The authors are experienced teachers or lecturers who are committed to bridging the gap between the huge body of research available to the more advanced student and what new students actually need to get them started on their studies.

Probably the most characteristic feature of communication is its diversity: it ranges from the mass media and popular culture through language to individual and social behaviour. But it identifies links and a coherence within this diversity. The series will reflect the structure of its subject. Some books will be general, basic works that seek to establish theories and methods of study applicable to a wide range of material; others will apply these theories and methods to the study of one particular topic. But even these topic-centred books will relate to each other, as well as to the more general ones. One particular topic, such as advertising or news or language, can only be understood as an example of communication when it is related to, and differentiated from, all the other topics that go to make up this diverse subject.

The series, then, has two main aims, both closely connected. The first is to introduce readers to the most important results of contemporary research into communication together with the theories that seek to explain it. The second is to equip them with appropriate methods of study and investigation which they will be able to apply directly to their everyday experience of communication.

If readers can write better essays, produce better projects and pass more exams as a result of reading these books I shall be very satisfied; but if they gain a new insight into how communication shapes and informs our social life, how it articulates and creates our experience of industrial society, then I shall be delighted. Communication is too often taken for granted when it should be taken to pieces.

John Fiske

Preface

This second edition of *Film as Social Practice* emerges from the perception that film and cultural theory has moved on appreciably since the first edition. And while this book looks at film theory from a cultural studies perspective, thus dealing with it in slightly different ways to most film textbooks, there were certain theoretical developments which it seemed necessary to deal with at greater length in this second edition. Foremost among these are the debates around audience and spectatorship and, most particularly, work within feminist film theory about 'the male gaze': the masculine nature of the narrative and visual pleasures offered by popular cinema. It has not been possible to greatly expand the length of the volume, and so the insertion of new material has had to be limited. However, I am confident that the revision has widened the range of ideas covered, and brought the ideas already dealt with up to date.

Among the aims of the first edition of *Film as Social Practice* was to provide an introduction to the study of film which placed it among the representational forms and social practices of popular culture. One of the ways in which this was done was to make substantial use of contemporary examples, drawing upon recent popular cinema as well as upon the 'classics' continually revisited in film courses. The first edition was completed in 1987, so its examples are much less contemporary now than when first used. In this revision, I have updated many of these examples, and also modified the arguments in places to account for the changing trends in contemporary cinema. My hope is that it is a more accessible, fresh and useful book as a consequence.

Graeme Turner, Brisbane, 1993

Introduction

In 1896 the French brothers Auguste and Louis Lumière became the first to project moving film to an audience. Like other pioneers in film, such as Thomas Edison in the USA, the Lumières imagined that their work with moving pictures would be directed towards scientific research rather than the establishment of an entertainment industry. Edison claimed that he decided to leave the movie industry as soon as its potential as a 'big amusement proposition' became clear, although his career makes this difficult to accept since he employed some cut-throat business practices. It is certainly true that when Edison ran his first 50 feet of film in 1888, the future he envisaged for moving pictures was more akin to what we now know as television; the emphasis was to be on domestic, information-based usage. However, despite the inappropriateness of the pioneers' initial objectives, it took barely fifteen years into the twentieth century for the narrative feature to establish itself – both as a viable commercial product and as a contender for the status of the 'seventh art', the new century's first original art form.

The history of film and of the ways in which it has been studied has already been written from a multitude of perspectives: as a narrative of key films, stars, and directors; as a story of ever-improving technology and more realistic illusions; as an industrial history of Hollywood and the multinational corporations which have succeeded it; as a cultural history, in which film is used as a reflector or index of movements within twentieth-century popular culture. And yet film studies have largely been dominated by one perspective – aesthetic analysis in which film's ability to become art through its reproduction and arrangement of sound and images is the subject of attention. This book breaks with this tradition in order to study film as entertainment, as narrative, as cultural event. The book is intended to introduce students to film as a social practice, and the understanding of its production and consumption, its pleasures and its meanings, is enclosed within the study of the workings of culture itself.

The academic area of film studies is now institutionalized in colleges, schools, and universities around the world. While there has always been a theoretical and academic interest in film, this interest expanded dramatically in the 1960s and 1970s – particularly in the USA, where film departments proliferated. The success of these departments can be deduced from the fact that the place once occupied by literature in humanities or arts courses is now challenged by film – just as the arts course is itself under attack from communications, media studies, or cultural studies courses of one kind or another.

Such challenges to the traditional literature or arts programme are, ironically, partly due to the defection of literature scholars who moved into the area of film studies during this period. While this has resulted in the increased sophistication of the understanding of film as a medium, the influence of attitudes developed in literary studies but applied to a popular and less verbal medium has not always been positive. Many literary scholars brought with them assumptions which later film theory was to challenge: for instance, a high-culture suspicion of such popular cultural forms as mainstream movies, television, or popular fiction; an exaggerated respect for the single unique text (book or film) coexisting with a patronizing attitude towards 'commercial', genre-styled films (westerns, thrillers, musicals, etc.); and a preference for films made from literary works. Interest in film in the 1960s and 1970s was rather narrowly circumscribed by the preference for modernistic, abstract films which bore greater similarities to literary works than to the mainstream of commercial feature film entertainment. Because film was seen to be analogous to literature, many of the things it did which literature did not were ignored. In particular, film's ability to attract millions of paying customers was disregarded because of aesthetic criticism of the most successful films. As a result it has taken some time to recover the need to understand the attraction of film-going itself: to understand the dreamlike separation from the everyday world that lies behind the shock we experience as we leave the cinema, or the lure of the luminous images on the screen.

The arguments which dominate most traditional texts on film

theory revolve around the formalism/realism debate (that is, whether or not to talk about film by way of its artistic – 'formal' – unity or by way of its specific relation to the particular world it is attempting to capture within its frames – its 'realism'). It is a debate which has a history as long as that of the medium itself, although its terms do keep changing. In their traditional form, rooted in arguments from the 1940s and 1950s, both the realist and formalist positions are aesthetic in that they are finally interested in evaluating how successful a film is as *art*, rather than as a social activity for its audience. There has, however, been a change in the kind of approach taken in film studies in the last fifteen years, and the movement away from a predominantly aesthetic approach is one that informs this book.

It is now more or less accepted that film's function in our culture goes beyond that of being, simply, an exhibited aesthetic object. Popular film takes place in an arena where the audience's pleasure is a dominant consideration – both for the audience and for the film's producers. This does not necessarily mean that the audience is drugged or fed 'junk food for the mind'. The pleasure that popular film provides may indeed be quite different from that offered by literature or fine art; it is, however, equally deserving of our understanding. Film provides us with pleasure in the spectacle of its representations on the screen, in our recognition of stars, styles, and genres, and in our enjoyment of the event itself. Popular films have a life beyond their theatre runs or their reruns on television; stars, genres, key movies become part of our personal culture, our identity. Film is a social practice for its makers and its audience; in its narratives and meanings we can locate evidence of the ways in which our culture makes sense of itself. Such is the view of film explored through these pages.

The following chapters are not comprehensive guides to the full body of film theory, but a map pointing out those areas of film and cultural theory that will be of most use to students first encountering the study of film – as a set of texts and as a social practice. Suggestions for further reading and consideration will follow each chapter, and point towards issues or applications I have been unable to include within the body of the text. Chapter 7 presents a set of sample analyses or 'readings' of films in order to demonstrate the kinds of approaches outlined earlier in the book. The aim is not to define what each film is 'about', or what it means, but to show what kind of information is produced by each analytical method. Throughout the book, but especially here, I am concerned with the *readings* any film may invite, rather than *the reading* we might want to impose.

In choosing examples with which to illustrate the points made in this book, I have attempted to deal primarily with mainstream, popular films which students may well have seen. Although there are references to some of the 'classic' films – *Metropolis* and *Citizen Kane*, for instance – the focus of this book is on film's function within popular culture, rather than its more rarefied role as high art. This is a film text about 'movies' *and* 'cinema', not just cinema alone. (Readers will note that such terms as film, movie, and cinema are used interchangeably throughout.)

In writing this book, I have received help and encouragement from a number of colleagues who deserve thanks. Most importantly, Bruce Molloy from the Queensland University of Technology, who was originally to be part of this project and had to withdraw, is owed particular thanks for his contribution to the early planning and design of the book. Other colleagues who read sections – Dugald Williamson from Griffith University and Stuart Cunningham from Queensland University of Technology – and my ever encouraging friend and editor John Fiske from the University of Wisconsin, Madison also deserve gratitude for their patience and interest. My research assistant, Shari Armistead, who searched out most of the illustrations with charm and determination, relieved me of an unpleasant task and has made a significant contribution to the book. None of the above are, of course, responsible for any flaws the reader may detect in this book.

Chapter 1

The feature film industry

THE FEATURE FILM TODAY

The role of the feature film within western cultures may no longer be as pronounced as it was in the 1930s, but it is still pervasive. Now, popular film is rarely presented to its public as a single product or commodity. It can be a kind of composite commodity, incorporating the *Wayne's World* T-shirt or the *Terminator* doll into the purchase of the cinema ticket. Film is no longer the product of a self-contained industry but one of a range of cultural commodities produced by large multinational conglomerates whose main interest is more likely to be electronics or petroleum than the construction of magical images for the screen.

Going to see a film is still an event, however, the nature of which will be discussed in Chapter 5. But it is not a discrete event. As film audiences have declined, and the pressure on producers to compete for these shrinking audiences has increased, many changes in industry practices have occurred. These changes have serially affected an individual film's place in its cultural context. First, the industry's concentration on the blockbuster – the expensive movie with high production values, big stars, and massive simultaneous release – has made it harder for more modest films to gain publicity or even distribution. Despite frequent examples of these more modest films succeeding at the box-office – *Home Alone*, for a recent instance – the industry has been particularly cautious in choosing projects to support. As a result, it has become more difficult for an independent producer to interest a major company in backing his or her film. During the 1980s, this actually helped to provide opportunities for producers of 'teen movies', which have good box-office potential but, usually, lower production costs. Such opportunities were few in other genres, however, as the concentration on the blockbuster reduced the variety of films produced while increasing the competition for, and thus the fees paid to, the few 'bankable' stars. (This trend, by 1992, seems to have peaked and may even be in decline.) The second change in industry practices, itself a sign of the commercial pressures on the producer-distributors, is the tendency to provide enormous levels of marketing support for those few films chosen as the likely hits of the season. These hits are backed up with merchandizing (the *Teenage Mutant Ninja Turtle* dolls), tie-ins (a hit single, for instance, like 'Unchained Melody' from *Ghost*), and the full range of advertising and promotional strategies – giveaways, competitions, dissemination of logos and so on.

The desire to watch a popular film is related to a whole range of other desires – for fashion, for the new, for the possession of icons or signs that are highly valued by one's peers. For example, in most countries T-shirts with the logo for *Ghostbusters* were ubiquitous well before the film was released; so was the hit single. As advertising for *Ghostbusters* they did not need to represent an accurate image of the experience of the film. Their job was to put the film on the list of 'new' commodities to be tried. The Bryan Adams hit single '(Everything I Do), I Do It For You' carried a quite different story to the film it accompanied, *Robin Hood*, but it (and the supporting video) helped to promote the desire to see the film. Marketing has recognized that film is now part of a multi-media complex. We have seen the expansion of the marketing of products more or less associated with a film, the sales of both products 'tied in' to each other. Probably the most elaborate array of tie-ins was that surrounding the 1979 film, *Jaws*; this included a sound-track album, T-shirts, plastic tumblers, a book about the making of the movie, the book the movie was based on, beach towels, blankets, shark costumes, toy sharks, hobby kits, iron-on transfers, games, posters, shark's tooth necklaces, sleepwear, water pistols, and more.

Advertising budgets have grown, not only in response to the fall in audiences but also to the change in the nature of their use of the cinema. At the peak of the feature film's popularity, audiences attended their favourite cinema as a regular night out – often more than once a week – and regardless of what was showing. Going to *the movies* was the event, not going to *this particular* movie. That situation has now reversed itself as home-based competitors for

1 The sequel – a sign of a cautious industry. Michael Keaton and Danny DeVito in *Batman Returns*

the entertainment dollar have appeared – cable TV, VCRs, video games, stereos, home computers – and as the increased mobility of the population – a result of the spread of private vehicle ownership – has multiplied the leisure-time choices available to any one individual. A film has to attract its own audience if it is to be successful. In many cases advertising budgets are larger than the production budget: *The Omen*, for instance, was made for US$3 million and had a promotion budget of US$6 million. It has been estimated that the average amount needed to promote a major studio release in America is now around $8 million and is going up all the time.

A further cost which is now built into the industry, although only for major pictures, is the cost of releasing the film simultaneously in a large number of cinemas and cities. An opening in as many as 1,000 cities simultaneously provides so much publicity – even news, as its scale turns the release into an event – that the picture is more visible, more talked about. If the audience like it, the interest generated can be considerable. 'If' is the operative word, of course, since none of these marketing strategies can guarantee success. *The Great Gatsby*, for instance, was released in 1973 on a large scale, with tie-ins, a famous novel to deliver its audience, and two highly 'bankable' (i.e. safe box-office money-makers) stars in Mia Farrow and Robert Redford. It flopped.

As costs have risen, as big budgets for production and for promotion have become the norm, American domination of feature film production and distribution in the English-speaking world has become further entrenched. Only major companies can now afford current production and promotion costs. America is still the biggest single market for feature films and it is one of the very few countries where locally produced films can recoup their costs without relying on foreign sales. Even Britain's population cannot support any more than the most modest locally produced film. It does, however, provide a juicy market where an American film which has already covered its costs at home can be distributed cheaply in order to generate profits. The integration between the production and the distribution arms of the film industry in America means that foreign-made films find it very hard to reap similar benefits from the lucrative American market. For a foreign film to achieve mainstream distribution in the US it would need to be supported by a major distributor whose *own* films are the main competitors to any foreign product. It is clearly not often in the major's interests to support its competitors.

The difference in size between the American and other major markets for English-language films – and thus the economies of scale which can be employed – is dramatically underlined by the release pattern employed by the American major, Paramount, which distributed the Australian film *Crocodile Dundee* in 1986. The first Australian film to be picked up by a major in this way, it was given a high-profile release, opening in 900 cinemas across the USA on the same night. That is 200 more cinemas than exist in the *whole* of Australia. In twelve days in the US the film earned what it had taken six months to earn in Australia although it had already become the biggest box-office success in Australian history!

Films may not have changed, in that their audiences still find the same kind of pleasure in them that they always have; but the industry has changed. Once a small-scale business run by enthusiastic entrepreneurs, it became concentrated into an oligopoly run by Hollywood studios. Now they, too, have had to sell out to other interests – in communication and electronics, mainly – so film is now simply another result of the large conglomerates' need to diversify. While the activities on the sound stages and the locations may still be those of the craftsperson, the economic practices of the industry are those of big business. This has alienated a number of film-makers, and fostered rhetoric about the death of the film industry. Independent film maker Robert Altman is characteristic in his views:

> You couldn't get me out of the house to see an American film; the artists have left it and it's being run by bookkeepers and insurance people, and all they're concerned with is the lowest common denominator so they can sell the most tickets. They don't try to produce anything but the sort of mass audience film that brings in a hundred million dollars, and that's all they're shooting for.
>
> (Hamilton 1986: 44)

That anyone should be interested in Altman's view, and people are (Altman's 1992 film, *The Player*, has been a success *because* of its dramatization of this view), suggests that the situation is not as bad as he claims; but there is, as we shall see, some truth to the claim that the industry is going through major changes at the moment. In order to understand these changes we need to gain

2   Cinemas in the nineties: the multiplex, offering a menu of movies

some idea of what the industry has been, and how it reached its present set of practices, conditions, and objectives.

THE ESTABLISHMENT OF THE FEATURE FILM

The feature film was not firmly established as the main attraction in the cinema until the introduction of optical sound with *The Jazz Singer* in 1927. Until then, the larger cinemas supported the features with an orchestra, vaudeville, or some other kind of live musical entertainment. A significant portion of the theatre-owner's costs went on providing such performances. After the establishment of the talking picture the practice of hiring support-ing entertainment gradually disappeared from the industry.

Although it is tempting to see the development of sound and its application to the film industry as a natural, inevitable develop-ment, it is a temptation we should resist. First, the technology to produce sound was in existence well before it was applied. So we need to ask 'Why *then*?' Second, technological innovation does not produce a momentum all of its own. As Ed Buscombe (1977: 83) points out 'no new technology can be introduced unless the econ-omic system requires it', and even then it will not be successful 'unless it fulfils some kind of need'. By 'need' he means some cultural, aesthetic, or political need, not just a perceived economic need. Changes in technology may be produced by individual in-ventors but their large-scale adoption depends on a wide range of other enabling cultural conditions. While the history of the feature film has often been written as a history of technological develop-ment, we need to be aware that even the term 'development' implies that by going from silent film to sound film we have made an advance. This implication, as we shall see shortly, depends upon debatable assumptions about what a film should be, includ-ing the assumption that it should be as 'realistic' as possible. There has been a great deal of argument over the industrial reasons for the introduction of sound. One view has it that the Hollywood majors were in financial trouble; audiences were declining and the mid-1920s expansion into the extravagant 'picture palaces' had saddled the industry with a string of venues which could only return a profit from the most popular of movies. Warner Bros, the first to use optical sound in a series of shorts and then in the musical, *The Jazz Singer*, are claimed to have been facing bank-ruptcy anyway, and clinging to the hope of the talking picture like a drowning man (Sklar, 1975). Douglas Gomery (1976) denies this view, saying that Warners were not bankrupt at all. He sees their achievement in the introduction of sound as a prescient business decision. At the time, Warners were not one of the major companies and had trouble competing. What they needed was, in effect, a new product that none of the others had. Sound was that product.

Whatever the truth of the industrial history, there were some aesthetic and ideological conditions supporting the introduction of sound which deserve consideration. As Buscombe (1977) says, there has to be a specific need satisfied for a technological change to be successful. The need he identifies in the advent of sound is the need for the narrative feature film to become more realistic. The development of the moving picture from the still camera was a movement towards realism, towards the apparent replication of the experience of viewing life. Such an account argues that the camera itself is an apparatus that embodies a theory of reality, an ideology, because it sees the world as the object of a single individual's point of view. We claim to see and possess the world as individuals – a view not held before the Renaissance but increasingly demonstrated in nineteenth-century art and entertainment. As Steve Neale (1985: 22) argues, there is nothing natural or inevitable about this way of seeing or its instruments, such as the camera: 'Photography . . . constituted an enormous social investment in the centrality of the eye, in the category and identity of the individual, in a specific form of visual pleasure, and in an ideology of the visibility of the world.'

Neale argues that photography and the camera had a democratic effect. Just as film is more democratic than the theatre, photographs of loved ones were cheap and accessible equivalents of the family portraits in the rich man's gallery. However one views such arguments, it is clear that the increasingly realistic reproduction of the world offered by the camera must be embedded in the ideological and aesthetic systems of the nineteenth century.

The introduction of sound also facilitated the complication of realistic narrative in films. Here realism is not just an ideological position, but an explicit aesthetic – a set of principles of selection and combination employed in composing the film as a work of art. The reproduction of dialogue reconnected the feature film with real life, and the industry rapidly developed a system of conventions for shooting and cutting dialogue. For instance, the technique of shot-reverse shot over a continuous sound-track was used to represent a conversation. (In this convention the characters speaking to each other appear on opposite sides of successive frames, each looking in the direction of the other.) Such conventions helped complete the evolution of the system we now use as we watch and construct a narrative feature film. These systems are analogous to those employed in the nineteenth-century novel, the epitome of realistic art. Certainly, the feature film, like the realist novel, sets out to construct a realistic world, to provide psychological depth for its characters, and to place itself within notions of real life. This series of objectives dominates the development of the narrative feature after the advent of sound.

In contrast to such ideological and aesthetic considerations, a persuasive explanation for the introduction of sound as an economic strategy relies on its effectiveness in reviving a dwindling cinema audience. In the US between 1927 and 1929, net profits for exhibition companies rose by 25 per cent; for production companies they rose a massive 400 per cent. This, despite the high cost of converting to sound in production and exhibition. However, one still has to resist such a simple cause-and-effect explanation in mapping cultural change. Colour provides a cautionary example of the failure of new technology to hold an audience. Far from increasing cinema audiences, it proved to be a relatively costly and unpopular process until the introduction of colour television. More on this later in the chapter.

It is undeniable that one of the effects of, if not the motivation for, the introduction of sound was the re-establishment of Hollywood's hegemony over world markets. Both the German and the Russian industries were aesthetically and culturally influential in the late 1920s and were looming as competitors in the quality of their films, if not in their ability to market them. Hollywood, being the first on the block with sound, outstripped these rivals. The advantage was reinforced by the development of a new genre, the musical, which to this day is still a quintessentially American form. The great virtue of the musical – apart from its obvious exploitation of sound – was that it could offer the pleasures of film and vaudeville at the same time. Many famous artists, never likely to share the same vaudeville bill, could be seen on the one screen. It was very difficult for foreign industries to compete with this.

A further industrial effect of the move into sound was that it changed the nature of the financial backing for the industry in the USA. To finance the transfer to sound, the film industry had to go outside its own boundaries, into the world of the Wall Street bankers and into the communication industry – the location of sound technology. Although this may not have appeared to be such a dramatic move, its long-term effects on the evolution of the industry have been profound. While these effects may have been localized, the story of the feature film industry is inevitably tied up with American domination, and movements within the American industry affect all the others. To gain some understanding of this we need to take a further step back, into the period before the end of the silent feature film.

AMERICAN DOMINATION OF THE FEATURE FILM INDUSTRY

The projection of moving pictures for commercial purposes began in France and the French film industry maintained its dominance over the world market until the First World War. Pathé Frères was the world's largest film producer until this time, supplying up to 40 per cent of the films released in the United Kingdom, for instance, as against America's 30 per cent. Other national cinemas were also thriving. The Italians supplied 17 per cent of the British market before the war (note how little this left for British features) and Australia had a sufficiently strong industry to produce multi-reel features regularly.

With the onset of war, the French and Italian industries cut their production dramatically, as did the less important industries in Britain and Germany. America moved into markets hitherto dominated by other suppliers – not only in Europe but also in Latin America (previously dominated by the French) and Japan (previously Italian-dominated). The results were dramatic. American film exports rose from 36 million feet in 1915 to 159 million in 1916; by the end of the war the US was said to produce 85 per cent of the world's movies and 98 per cent of those shown in America. The control of the US home market was most important, because movies could now be confidently made for an American market and sold abroad for profit. From this point on there has been little incentive for American producers to tailor their product for other than an American audience.

The first twenty years of commercial moving picture exhibition saw a rapid development of feature production and exhibition world-wide, followed by the expansion and domination of US-based companies. As the audiences for the cinema reached saturation point around 1922, and as competitors for the audience's leisure time began to appear – radio and the motor vehicle, for instance – the pressure on the minor producers increased. American domination had expanded during the classic silent period – for good reasons, since they made their films well – to the point where other national cinemas found their very survival threatened. In Australia in 1914 the USA supplied around 50 per cent of the films shown; in 1923 it supplied around 94 per cent. In Britain, the local share of the market had dwindled from a peak of around 15 to 20 per cent to a mere 5 per cent in 1926.

Capitalizing on the insurance of a large home market, American companies used their new dominance to change the structure of the industry. Once, production of films, their distribution to cinemas, and the management of cinemas exhibiting them were separate enterprises. As the American domination grew, it became apparent that control over the industry could be guaranteed if a company could produce, distribute, and screen its own movies. This change in structure, called vertical integration, began after the First World War. Throughout the 1920s Paramount, Loew's, Fox, and Goldwyn embarked on programmes of expansion, integration, and, most importantly, acquisition of first-run theatres in the major cities. Restrictive practices, such as Paramount's block booking, followed. Block booking enabled producers to extract agreement from exhibitors to take all their pictures in a total package, sight unseen, thus guaranteeing a screening for their product and making the exhibitor bear much of the risk for the film's success or failure. This practice was eventually outlawed in the US in 1948, and later in most other countries, but it exercised an important influence over the nature and conduct of the industry into the 1920s. It still survives in the way that old movies are sold to TV today.

One effect of vertical integration was to expand the capital base of the companies, as they drew investment from banks and communication companies in the push to expand. As this development continued, outside assistance became necessary, carrying with it affiliations, obligations, and responsibilities which rendered the movie industry vulnerable to movements in the financial markets during the Depression. Ultimately the industry became a hostage to these markets.

A further effect was to encourage the development and entrenchment of the studio system which had begun before the 1920s. The studio system was another method of control over the production and marketing of feature films. If studios could guarantee release for their pictures through their own distribution and exhibition network it made economic sense to put the most popular actors on an exclusive contract and retainer as a kind of repertory company. The development of the star system, the identification of studios with certain kinds of film, and the studio's control over directors, were possible because the production companies could determine whether a film would ever be screened, and whether it would be in New York or Peoria. There was little future for film industry workers outside the studio system.

Finally, competitors like the smaller Warners studio were shut out of these structures, and this ultimately led to the series of decisions which brought sound to the feature film. (Also, sound further entrenched the studio system as it made location shooting more difficult and 'sound stages' in studios became necessary.) The coming of sound initially tightened Hollywood's grip on the world cinema market. However, this only served to foster the adoption of vertical integration in other countries, linking national productions with distribution and exhibition chains so as to counteract American and German competition. Both France and Britain adopted this strategy. Britain set up a link between distribution, exhibition, and local production companies by including British International and Gaumont in the two conglomerates – Gaumont British and Associated British. Such strategies were sufficiently successful for British companies to engage in some offshore involvements. British Empire Films bought into the Greater Union share of the distribution and exhibition networks in Australia, and British commercial interests have been a feature of the Australian industry structure since the 1920s.

It has been suggested that after the novelty of sound dissipated, the US share of the international market declined. Clearly, sound introduced the problem of translation, and the pleasure of sound was obviously going to be minimal if foreign-language subtitles were needed. So locally made films had an advantage in countries where English was not the national language. This factor did open up space for some foreign industries, many of which were already sheltering behind a quota system limiting the number of films which could be imported or, more ingeniously, requiring an exporting nation to reciprocate by distributing the local product in their home market.

The 1930s, then, while a period of classic film-making, was not the healthiest for the Hollywood studios. As the Depression deepened, movie attendances dropped (by 30 per cent in 1932), and some companies went into receivership as a result of the debts owed to bankers and the large corporations during the conversion to sound. Fox, RKO, and Universal were all in this situation, and the influence of the financial managers can be seen to expand during this period. Despite the involvement of such business acumen, audiences did not recover until the economy did, well into the 1940s. Within this shrinking market national cinemas showed signs of establishing themselves again, particularly in Britain through the documentary movement. However, the recovery of the European film industries was short-lived. Once again it was interrupted by the outbreak of war.

During the war, the US regained some of its lost markets; it also began producing films in other countries, notably in Latin America. The big shake-up for the industry, foreshadowed in 1938 in the first challenge to vertical integration, came after the war when the practice was outlawed by the US Supreme Court. Exhibition was separated from production and distribution by the ruling of 1948, providing a model for other countries to follow – although some did not do so until well into the 1970s. Distribution, it was quickly realized, is the pivotal point of the film industry, and most production companies were careful to retain their distribution arms while dissolving their formal connections with exhibition. Distribution – gaining access to the right cinemas in sufficient numbers, and at the right time – is still the key to a film's success. Small national cinemas deal with this fact daily, as they try to find a suitable outlet for their films in competition with the big multinationals whose constant supply of product persuades the major exhibitors to deal more or less exclusively with them. Examples of chances missed – potential box-office hits being overlooked because they were made independently – are legion. When Australia's industry revived in the 1970s, the film which proved to be the catalyst – it showed Australian films could make money – could not find a distributor in its home country. *The Adventures of Barry McKenzie* eventually opened in a Melbourne cinema hired by the producers, and its successful run there had to be cut so that the exhibitor could meet its commitment to imported product. One of Britain's most successful post-war features, *Tom Jones*, failed to get a local circuit release initially, although it eventually went on to take one of the largest box-office grosses of 1963.

Since the demise of widespread vertical integration and the studio system, the role of the feature film has been under continual attack from new forms of entertainment, new financial constraints, and a fluctuating but generally declining audience. We are by no means witnessing the end of the feature film (in fact, its audiences are returning in encouraging numbers at the time of writing), but its cultural hegemony as the twentieth century's predominant form of entertainment is over. It is to the alternatives, and the feature film's response to these alternatives since the war, that we now turn.

NEW COMPETITORS, NEW STRATEGIES

In most western capitalist countries the figures for attendances at the movies peaked in 1946 and the overall trend has been downward ever since. By 1953, when nearly half of all American households had a TV set, the US attendance levels had sunk to half the 1946 figures. Quota systems in Britain, France, and Italy made it more difficult for American producers to recoup losses overseas, although one response to this – making American films in foreign studios – did cut costs and evaded some of the more stringent restrictions.

Although this decline in film audiences began before TV hit the largest market, America, television was obviously implicated in the complex of conditions which produced the trend. No one has yet satisfactorily explained why the decline occurred; but it is clear that film was already losing its cultural pre-eminence by the beginning of the 1950s and that TV merely exacerbated this decline. Reasons so far offered for this trend range from the fanciful – the baby boom kept parents at home looking after their (presumably booming) babies – to the sensibly economic – that the industry's response of making bigger and more expensive movies to win back its audience initiated a cycle of events which ultimately deepened the crisis. Surveys of Hollywood's production in the late 1940s also support the view that the industry had lost its identification with 'middle America' and the pictures it was making were less commercial. Whatever the reason, the threat of TV and the film industry's response to this threat seem to be crucial to this period of the industry's history.

The film industry responded to the threat of TV in two main ways. Of these, the attempt to 'colonize' TV by producing films for it has proved to be the more successful. The big media conglomerates which have prospered are those which have incorporated a TV production company, such as Gulf and Western's Paramount and Desilu. TV's enormous appetite for material meant that there was a large market to be developed and for the most part it was successfully developed by film producers. Warner Bros and Disney are examples of how successful the film industry's invasion of TV can be.

The less successful response is perhaps the more interesting. The experience of the conversion to sound had led the film industry to form some misconceptions about the relationship between technological innovations and box-office returns. This, combined with the attempt to make movies better than ever (and thus better than TV), produced some well-calculated, and some bizarre, innovations. A series of wide-screen formats appeared in the early 1950s: Cinerama was introduced in 1952, Cinemascope in 1953. Neither idea was new. Both dated from the 1920s. Cinerama used three projectors to screen images from three cameras on a curved screen in a specially equipped theatre. Cinemascope was cheaper and simpler, projecting its image onto an elongated screen, its dimensions not the prevailing 1.33:1, but 2.35:1. Both these screen formats have survived, and the normal size for projection screens is now wider than it was in the 1950s as a result of the success of these wide-screen formats. Neither process, however, was sufficiently dramatic to draw an audience singlehandedly. Cinerama was expensive to shoot and screen, and was largely seen in a series of demonstration films with roller-coaster rides and car chases which exploit the realistic effect produced by the wrap-around screen. It did not make the transition to narrative features, the only way to build and hold an audience. Cinemascope was more successful but, paradoxically, the greater success it had in carrying a narrative the less apparent was the technological innovation itself. It succeeded by becoming invisible rather than by appearing as a selling point.

Other attempts to build new experiences into the feature film during this period include 3-D (necessitating special spectacles and

3   3-D movie viewers, 1952 (photo by J. R. Eyerman, *Life Magazine*, ©
1970, Time Inc., used with permission)

two projectors operating simultaneously); and Aromarama and
Smel-O-Vision (both dependent, presumably, on plots with strong
smells). The latter two were gimmicks, involving a card impreg-
nated with smells which had to be activated by the user at certain
points in the film. Although these novelty processes are revived
periodically, their inherent silliness limited their impact on attendances. The only other venture to succeed was colour, but not
without difficulty.

Coloured movie film is not a recent invention. Several systems were in existence as early as 1900 and much silent film was tinted. Technicolor, the dominant producer/processor of coloured film stock for most of the 1930s and 1940s, was formed in 1915. One of the reasons why colour was not more widely used before the 1960s was the cost; some of the early processes were labour-intensive, early cameras were expensive, and Technicolor's eventual mono- poly often irritated and restricted producers. Colour was primarily used for spectacles, epics set in the past, or for special effects in fantasies. It became more widely used, though, after sound and Technicolor's introduction of a new three-colour subtractive process in 1932 (Steve Neale (1985) goes into this in more detail). The first to use this process was Walt Disney in his cartoon series, *Silly Symphonies*; other notable early users in the 1930s were Mamoulian in *Becky Sharp* and Selznick in *Gone with the Wind*. But it was not the dramatic breakthrough that sound had been and although its use increased steadily from the mid-1930s into the mid-1950s, it had nothing like the revolutionary effect of sound. This is even true of the 1950s after Eastmancolor had broken Technicolor's monopoly, reduced costs, and opened up space for a range of such new colour processes as Deluxe which were mobilized in the attempt to revive cinema attendances. It was not until TV's conversion to colour in the 1960s that colour film finally became the conventional stock for feature film production.

On the face of it, this is odd. Surely, the aim of the film is to replicate reality as closely as possible. If the advent of sound increased the film's correspondence with 'the real world', why not add colour? Ed Buscombe (1977: 88) offers an explanation:

> [This may] seem rather strange if one supposes that the demand for realism in the cinema has always been merely a question of the literal rendering of appearances. We perceive the world as coloured, after all, and therefore an accurate representation of it should also be coloured. . . . But in fact it has never been a question of what *is* real but what is *accepted* as real. And when it first became technically feasible, colour, it seems, did not connote reality but the opposite.

Colour was widely used in cartoons, musicals, westerns, and com- edies where fantasy or spectacle were paramount. So, colour's function was not to create the illusion of the real, but to signify artifice, decoration, the cinema as story-teller. In *The Wizard of Oz*, colour is used in the fantasy world of Oz, while the 'real' world of Dorothy's Kansas home is shot in black and white. As colour became part of current affairs programmes and news reporting on television it lost its association with fantasy and spectacle. The special ways in which colour was seen are useful reminders of how conventionalized our readings of film can be. Now, since colour has lost many of its unreal connotations it is hard to imagine that understanding of it. However, even now we can come across the residue of this way of seeing: black and white footage can still be used in documentary or in certain kinds of feature film (e.g. the Australian film *Newsfront*) as a guarantor of 'truth', the break into black and white signifying an amplification of the real. With such a history, then, colour never had much hope of reversing the decline in movie audiences in the way that sound had done.

One of the most important features of the decline in movie audiences has been the changes in their composition over the decades since the Second World War. The family market that once sustained the film industry has now all but gone, and in its place is a predominantly youthful market. The film industry now depends on pleasing the 14 to 24 age group. Going to the cinema is still a regular and highly valued leisure activity for this group, while the older middle-class audience, who were the new segment in the 1970s, are probably key contributors to the expansion of video and cable television. Market segmentation is the new premise; films are either aimed at a particular segment of the market – youth for instance – or are designed to contain within them attractions for a number of different market segments. The mass market has broken into smaller units, and the trend towards housing multiple cinemas under one roof – the multiplexes – reflects this. No longer can one film please the whole family – and the causes of this are not confined to the film industry – nor can one location expect to pay high overheads from the proceeds of exhibiting one film. A result has been the clearer definition of the new sub-genres, narratives developed for a specific segment of the market: *Star Wars* was perhaps the clearest example of the 'kidult' movie, aimed at two separate markets – the kids and their nostalgic parents; and the new youth movies, from *Porky's* to *The Breakfast Club* to *Wayne's World*, have established a market as well as a wide range of styles, content, and social/political attitudes.

This break-up of the mass market into smaller segments (which might be combined in the audience for specific films) followed an earlier segmentation. The introduction of alternative 'art-house' cinemas began in the 1950s and peaked in the 1970s. The art-house network took many different forms; in some countries it was subsidized by governments through such bodies as Britain's National Film Theatre, and in others it survived through subscriptions to 'seasons' from its patrons. It originally existed to screen non-American films – primarily European – and it contributed to the growth in respect accorded to the British and, more recently, the Australian film industries. In 1986, six out of the 'top ten' foreign films at the US box-office were British. The art-house circuit is now more properly seen as a kind of specialist, non-mainstream, or repertory cinema which presents new films made by independents as well as offering retrospective glances at classics and constructing 'seasons' or groups of films from a particular country, director, or movement, which will run over a set period.

An American representative of Cinecom, a minor distribution agency, describes the specialized film market in this way:

> The specialised film audiences are hard-core film fans – older, better educated, and skewed towards the female side. So it's a safer marketing situation than that dealt with by the majors where millions are thrown on a dice day after day. Our audiences are more specific, so you know immediately if you have a hit or a flop, and since our audience is so swayed by critical response, the critics influence it enormously.
>
> (Mathews 1986: 199)

It is clearly a very different business to mainstream film distribution. A film can open in one city, play it for weeks, and only then move to another city. Without a large advertising budget, films are dependent on critics' approval and recommendation by word of mouth from those who see them. The supply of 'art' films has diminished since the 1970s but this deficit has been more than met by the supply of films which are aimed at a mass audience but are either not American-made or for some other reason have not won the support of the major distributors. So, these days, a key function for the specialized film network is to provide outlets for all kinds of independents – from disillusioned American directors to mainstream but non-American films which may want to develop a case for major distribution. Many British and Australian films which have drawn mass audiences at home have been distributed through art-house or specialized cinemas in America. For most films made outside America, but still wishing to break into the lucrative American market, this is the best alternative after they have failed to convince a major distributor to take them on. Since it is very rare indeed for a major to take on a foreign film, it is also the most common method of distribution for independent films. It is a long way from the big profits, however. The six British films which were among the top ten foreign earners for 1986 in the US drew in only $30 million between them. At an average of $5 million per film, this is only the cost of a strong promotional campaign for a major release. It is better than nothing but it is a long way from success.

A final note here concerns other means of distributing film: through video sales and rental, and through cable television. Although the spread of VCR ownership has made the watching of video movies an important aspect of film industry practices, I should point out that it is still *television* that is being watched. So it is outside the scope of this book. It is worth noting, however, the importance of these two aspects of distribution and exhibition for the film industry as a whole. Video movie rentals are largely but not exclusively dependent upon the reputation that a film builds up in theatre exhibition; this seems to be true of most films outside the restricted horror and sex areas. Cable TV, though, does require an enormous amount of material to stay on the air, and channels which only screen movies are important buyers for films from both the majors and the independent production companies. One such organization, Home Box Office, has over 14 million subscribers in the US and is partially integrated with film production companies. HBO is now a key target for film-makers who wish to support a minor theatrical release with all the extras the industry can offer in order to return a profit. The gradual increase in the importance of HBO has begun, and will continue, to exercise some influence over the nature of film production and distribution in the US and, therefore, elsewhere.

Despite regular warnings of doom for the film industry – emanating from prognoses of the impact of VCRs, or from the development of high-definition television pictures – the feature film still offers a distinctive set of experiences, pleasures, and social practices for its audiences. None of the competitors has been able to replicate these. That film has survived is due to its nature as a medium, and its social usage by its audiences. Audiences enjoy going to the movies. To find out how, and perhaps even why, is the project for the rest of this book. We start by reviewing the study of

4   Cinema now offers the pleasures of TV in order to promote the pleasures of the movies

film, prior attempts to analyse the nature of the medium, and its appeal for an audience.

SUGGESTIONS FOR FURTHER WORK

1. Those interested in knowing more about the cultural development of the movies in the US could read Robert Sklar's *Movie-Made America* (1975), and for a history of the American hegemony in film see Kristin Thompson's *Exporting Entertainment* (1985).
2. The development of colour processes is beyond the range of this book but is worthy of further study. Steve Neale's *Cinema and Technology* (1985) provides a detailed analysis of the development of these processes as well as reproductions of stills using the different processes.
3. How do you see the relationship between your national cinema and the American movie? It could be interesting to discuss this with others, and see if the problems outlined in this chapter have occurred to anyone else.
4. The development of the cinema has increased the sophistication of audiences; some TV producers have maintained that TV advertising, for instance, has taught audiences to read films better and more quickly than ever before. Analyse a silent movie, and see what differences of convention and what differences in audience reaction you can locate between silents and talkies.
5. Discuss the attributes of a 'kidult' movie such as *Star Wars* or *E. T.* or *Home Alone*. What do you think is the attraction for the various age groups to such a film?
6. Do you think that there is such a thing as a 'youth' film – for example, the films of John Hughes, such as *Pretty in Pink* or *Ferris Bueller's Day Off*? If it does exist, how would you describe it?
7. Film production has become increasingly a part of multinational companies' pattern of investment. What effects are likely to flow from this? Thompson's *Exporting Entertainment* (1985) might help you to consider this problem.
8. For further work on film history, Allen and Gomery's *Film History: Theory and Practice* (1985) and Cook's *A History of Narrative Film* (1981) are both useful.

Chapter 2

From seventh art to social practice – a history of film studies

EARLY AESTHETIC APPROACHES

The beginnings of motion picture exhibition can be found in vaudeville, music-hall, amusement arcades, fairgrounds, and travelling shows. It commences almost simultaneously in France, Britain, and the USA. Commercial development of the technology began almost immediately after the first exhibitions. The French pioneers, the Lumières, sold their commercial interests to Charles Pathé in 1900, and this paved the way for large-scale commercial development and for initial domination by French film production. In France, the audience for the medium spread across the classes, but it remained working class for some time in the USA and Britain. In the US it began in penny arcades ('penny gaffs' in Britain) and in vaudeville houses as featured support to live acts, but within the first decade of exhibition it had moved into store-front theatres in, primarily, working-class neighbourhoods across America. In Australia, the travelling picture show man was also important, bringing his films to country towns and projecting them in local halls or marquees. In all cases, it was a medium that went as directly to its audience as possible.

The first films were not structured narratives, but brief one-shot recordings of everyday scenes, such as the Lumières' famous film of workers leaving their factory at the end of a shift. The models provided by vaudeville skits (performed in the same locations as the pictures were projected in) soon revealed what could be done with the addition of some fictional or comic structure. The brevity of these early films – some lasted for less than a minute – fitted music-hall 'sight' gags rather well and the link between the feature film and vaudeville was often explicit and direct.

The French producer George Méliès is usually credited with the development of the narrative feature film, and he commenced commercial production in 1896. His most important contribution was to free 'screen time' (the amount of time taken to project the film on to the screen) from 'real time' (the amount of time actually taken to perform the actions or complete the events depicted on the screen). We take it for granted now that a screen representation of a war which lasted five years does not actually take that long; early feature film, however, did not immediately grasp the possibility of intervening between the reality being filmed and its representation on the screen. Joining separate pieces of film – editing – made this intervention possible. The use of *editing* was pioneered by Méliès, and it enabled the film-maker to orchestrate the sequence of images on the screen rather than allowing this to be dictated by the subject matter itself. Méliès is also credited with the invention of other practices which made it possible for narratives to be structured – that is, speeded-up, slowed down, in short, composed – with some economy. Such techniques as the *fade-out* (the disappearance of the image into black) as a method of transition or closure, and the *lap-dissolve* (a fade-out coinciding with the gradual superimposition of a new image) as a more elegant method of transition, have assisted all narrative film-makers since. They are early examples of the development of techniques which became formalized into a system of conventions which determines both film-making practice and the audience's 'decoding' or understanding of the narrative as they watch it. We will talk more about these conventions and this process of decoding in later chapters.

The date of the first narrative feature film is a perennial source of nationalist argument; England, France, the USA, and Australia all have contenders. What *is* clear is that within ten years of the beginnings of production and exhibition in Europe and America, the feature film industry had established the concept of the narrative feature and the means of composing it through shots and editing, and the first western had been produced (*The Great Train Robbery* (1903)). This immediate success and rapid development are perhaps less surprising than the rapidity with which this form of mass entertainment came to be seen as a new aesthetic form, a companion to sculpture, painting, or literature: the 'seventh art'.

In 1915, two events occurred which are worth linking in that they represent a kind of turning-point for the place of film within western cultures. D. W. Griffith's *Birth of a Nation* was released to an extraordinary popular and critical response; in its epic scale (it was the longest feature so far) and the personal quality of its vision seemed to lie the potential of great art. The same year, 1915, also saw the publication of Vachel Lindsay's *The Art of the Moving Picture*. Whereas prior to *Birth of a Nation* movies had been the subject of middle-class condescension, Lindsay, an American poet, used his intelligent, prescient, and clearly polemical book to stake film's claim to the status of the seventh art form. With very little in the way of existing feature films to support his position, Lindsay announced his intention of convincing the cultural institutions of America that the 'motion picture is a great high art'. Lindsay was not the only one to hold such a view, and much of the theory which succeeds him for the next forty or fifty years happily accepts this proposition. While the legal and governmental discussion of film concentrates on issues of class, entertainment, and morality, much early film theory argues over the definitions of, or prescriptions for, the aesthetic characteristics of film.

Griffith's next film, *Intolerance* (1916), failed to repeat his popular and critical success and thus he lost some of his pre-eminence in the US as the film 'artiste'. However, his influence spread beyond America and was particularly strong in the 1920s in Germany and Russia. There, state-funded film industries were producing films into which 'the film-maker as artist' was clearly inscribed. German expressionism and Soviet montage were fashionable and respected as developments of film's aesthetic potential, and came close to challenging Hollywood's leadership in the formal development of the silent feature. There seems to have been a strong prejudice against local films among the American intelligentsia in the 1920s, and a strong preference for the more 'expressive' (that is, more clearly the statement of an artist) films from Europe.

The 'expressive' use of film is usually defined as the reshaping of the raw material printed on celluloid, using images of the real world to 'make a statement'. The images become something else, art. Like the nineteenth-century novel, the expressive film sets out to create *its own* world rather than simply reproduce the one we know. Possibly the most important of the figures exploiting the potential of film as an expressive art at this time was the Russian exponent of montage, Sergei Eisenstein.

Eisenstein is an influential figure, and a customary starting-point for histories of film technique and film theory. As a theorist,

Eisenstein is notable for attempting to understand the language of film. As a film-maker, he used editing as his major tool to transform exposed film into a statement. According to his theory, the meaning of film is produced by the audience's contrasting or comparing the two shots which make up a montage (the physical joining together of two separate shots by splicing the film). Eisenstein was not interested in simply reproducing the reality he had filmed; he wanted to use the images he had filmed to create something new. As he saw it, two film pieces of any kind, placed together, inevitably combine into a new concept, a new quality arising out of the juxtaposition. That new quality is constructed by the viewer. So, one shot of a face, followed by another of a loaf of bread, might create the idea of hunger through the *combination* of shots. The meanings generated by montage are more than the sum of their parts, and the editing technique which produces montage is the basic structuring technique behind film composition.

The idea that film simply recorded or reproduced images of the real world came under attack here. Instead, film was proposed as a medium which can *transform* the real, and which has its own language and its own way of making sense. And as far as this went, it was accurately understood. Montage *does* work as Eisenstein suggested; as a tool of Soviet education it was effective, its didacticism a political benefit. An irony is that its most common use in contemporary capitalist societies now is in advertising; this irony is lessened a little by the fact that it is also widely used in rock music video clips. As we shall see, however, when we deal with subsequent critiques of Eisenstein and montage, it is only one way of communicating through film, not the basis of its language.

Eisenstein was not alone in his rejection of any view of film that would relegate it to the category of a simple recording agent. A number of theorists argued, in fact, that the very *limitations* of film as a recording agent were the factors which determined its artistic potential. Although many such positions are expressive, the extreme aestheticism which underlies them separates them from Eisenstein. When sound comes to the movies in 1927, such theories emerge in something of a rush. Rudolph Arnheim's *Film as Art* (1958, first published in 1933) is only one such argument which sees the silent film as a superior medium for aesthetic purposes; for Arnheim, the silent film's inability to reproduce the world entirely realistically is the source of its artistic potential. The idea that art is an imitation of the real, a conventional literary and aesthetic tenet,

5 Eisenstein's *Battleship Potemkin* (courtesy of the National Film and Sound Archive of Australia)

is denied in order to propose film's special qualities as an art form. A by-product of such arguments was an attack on the 'lust for the complete illusion' of sound and colour on the movie screen. Realism and art were thus placed in opposition to each other with the silent film being given the status of art while the sound film was dismissed as crass and vulgar.

Such approaches as we have been examining in the last few pages are usually considered under the label of 'formalism' in film histories. Formalist approaches see a film's forms of representation (its specific manipulation of vision and sound) as more important in the production of meaning than its 'content' or subject matter. The dubious distinction between form and content is thus blurred by the assertion that the form *is* the content. Formalism is an approach which examines the film text for its own intrinsic interest, without necessitating reference to its realism or 'truth' to some version of the real world. Formalism is opposed to any view of film as the *capture* of the real world; instead it proposes film as a *transformation* of the real.

REALIST APPROACHES

The coming of sound to the feature film reinforced the trend towards greater realism of narrative form and structure which was already becoming apparent in the silent film. Sound was held to enhance greatly the illusion of reality. Further, within the individual film, the use of dialogue of some complexity and detail now made possible greater intricacies of motivation, more psychological versions of character, and complexities of tone such as irony or sarcasm. As pointed out in Chapter 1, the changes which followed the advent of sound were incorporated into the narrative feature's progressive imitation of the classic nineteenth-century novel, with its individualistic delineation of character, social world, and notions of personal and moral conflict.

If expressive or formalist views of film dominated the European silents, the advent of sound contributed to the conditions which favoured a revival of realism in European cinema after the Second World War. A further contributing factor may have been the brief burst of social realism in Hollywood films of the early 1930s (*Smart Money* (1931), *The Public Enemy* (1931), or *Scarface* (1932)) – a mode quickly scotched by the industry's self-censorship mechanisms. However, a key factor in the post-war interest in realist film

may well have been the success of the documentary movement in
the 1930s and 1940s initiated in the UK, and led by John Grierson.
The movement became known beyond the UK as documentary
units were set up in Canada and Australia with Grierson's assistance, and later as wartime documentaries were made and shown.
Now it is the most developed form of film-making after the narrative feature and probably the most respected.

This respect was won early. Under Grierson's leadership, the
documentary film was seen to offer a social service in dealing with
problems and issues of national importance (at a time, it might be
said, when there was an unusually high degree of consensus about
what was important). At the same time it offered itself as an
aesthetic object: Basil Wright and Harry Watt's *Night Mail* (1936),
for instance, has been representatively described as an 'aural and
visual poem to man, machine, and the work they perform' (Sobchack and Sobchack 1980: 345). The documentary movement had
a profound influence on British film, particularly the products of
Ealing Studios, during the next thirty years. Britain's achievement
of a reputation for 'quality' during the 1960s, a reputation largely
drawn from the modes of documentary realism employed in films
such as *This Sporting Life*, has had an influence on the social
realism in Hollywood films since. British television is probably
the major beneficiary of this tradition, though, with the realist
docu-drama (*Days of Hope, Boys from the Blackstuff*) becoming
recognizable as a British genre. The social impact of film is also
reinforced by the documentary movement, pushing aesthetics
to one side in the face of social movements and upheavals that
make art film seem a little self-indulgent. Such an effect is also
reinforced by the major realist movement of the period, the
'neo-realism' of the post-war Italian directors, Rossellini, de Sica,
and Visconti.

Neo-realist films look like documentary; they have a grainy,
under-lit look, rather than the evenly lit, glossy image of the classic
fictional film of the period. Neo-realists distrusted the use of
narrative as a contrived structuring device; they often dispensed
with actors and replaced them with 'real people' under the
assumption that this would be more true to life, and they made
extensive (for the time) use of location rather than studio shooting. The movement distanced itself as far as possible from the
staged confections of previous Italian films – the epics and the
sophisticated farces called 'white telephone' films – and dealt with

social and political issues affecting everyday life in occupied and post-war Italy. For Italians in the mid-1940s, everyday life was a more than sufficient subject, and the aim of the neo-realist cinema was to deal with it as directly as possible – to capture 'the illusion of the present tense', as one director put it (Cook 1981: 391).

Neo-realism is a film movement – a body of films loosely directed towards similar formal or social ends – as well as a theory of what the cinema should be as an art form. Although the movement died out within five or six years, its influence has been profound in suggesting what relations film might have to the real world. Its influence on the French New Wave of the 1950s and 1960s is widely acknowledged, and there are a number of significant Hollywood directors who admit to its influence. Industrially, it exposed new acting styles and revealed the greater possibilities of location shooting.

We have been talking about European films and film theory at a time when Europe was not the dominant force in world feature film production, distribution, or exhibition. The 1930s and 1940s are the heyday of Hollywood, of the star system. The war's gutting of the competing European cinemas of France, Italy, Germany, and Britain had once again left the market open to American domination. Yet much film theory of the time ignores Hollywood, and concentrates on the realist aesthetic being developed in Europe. Eventually, as we shall see, it is through the arguments around realism that the renovation of interest in Hollywood and in American popular film occurs.

BAZIN

André Bazin is the next key figure. Through his writings and his involvement with the French journal he founded in 1951, *Cahiers du Cinéma*, Bazin is seen as a centre of realist approaches to film. Although he never developed his position in fully argued form, he has been extremely influential. Firstly, he consigned Eisenstein to the past. In contrast to Eisenstein, who saw the intrinsic nature of film lying in the *combination* of shots, Bazin saw the intrinsic quality of film in the *composition* of the shot itself – its specific representation of the real world. For Bazin, it is the real world which is the subject of film art. For Eisenstein, shots were only raw material, the 'fragments of reality' constructed into art through montage. Bazin found montage too manipulative, too distorting of the real, too much of an imposition of the film-maker upon the viewer. Instead, as he saw it, the shot and, particularly, the long uninterrupted take allow the viewer to scan the frame, to read and interpret what it represented.

Bazin looked to the movement and arrangement of elements within the frame or the shot in order to examine how meaning might be generated. The movement and placement of figures, camera position, lighting, set design, the use of deep focus, all merit greater attention from this perspective. Significantly, all these features also enhance the illusion of reality and thus constitute the 'art' of the film. For Bazin, the real and the aesthetic were not separable. As Brian Henderson (1971b: 397) has said, for Bazin 'film art has no overall form of its own, but that of the real itself. Bazin has a theory of the real, he may not have an aesthetic.'

The term used to describe the arrangement of elements within the frame or the shot is *mise-en-scène*. The term itself has been more influential than Bazin's wider theories, possibly because it inspired the rejection of Eisenstein's claim to have established montage as the basis for a grammar of film composition. Further, the notion of *mise-en-scène* is useful in that it allows us to talk about the way in which elements within a frame of film, or a shot composed of many consecutive frames, are placed, moved, and lit. Since significance can be communicated without moving the camera or editing – for instance through a character moving closer to the camera, or throwing a shadow over another's face – the concept of *mise-en-scène* becomes an important means of locating the process through which such significance is communicated. It is also widely used as a means of analysis of visual style in particular films or groups of films. Today, montage and *mise-en-scène* are no longer seen as mutually exclusive terms, but are contained within a notional grammar of film language.

The shift from montage to *mise-en-scène* can be seen as a shift towards an emphasis on visual style. Most importantly, emphasis on the interpretative role of the viewer in *mise-en-scène* prefigures a reorientation in film theory. It eventually results in a revaluation of popular film; more significantly, it begins the movement away from an examination of the relations between film and reality and towards an examination of the relationship between film and the viewer.

AUTEURS AND GENRES

Auteur theory is usually credited with having given the feature film an 'author'. Instead of being a co-operative, industrial project, a film became identified with its director, who was seen as its ultimate creator. This is something of a distortion of the *auteur* position, but an understandable one because the *auteur* theory *does* attempt to insert an author – in the literary, expressive sense – into films which had hitherto been regarded as the faceless, standardized products of a studio system. As such it is an odd theory to discuss while charting the decline of aesthetics; nevertheless, in my view, that is where it belongs.

A polemical article by French film-maker François Truffaut, published in *Cahiers du Cinéma* in 1954, marks the beginning of *auteur* 'theory'. Although its specific points were almost entirely enclosed within industrial and political conflicts in the French film industry at the time, it led to a position which was aesthetic in that it argued for the necessity of a personal vision or style in a director's films; even some films produced under the most industrialized conditions (Hollywood) were held to bear the mark of an artist/*auteur*. As such, the theory invoked artistic standards while at the same time, paradoxically, rescuing a large body of popular films (Jerry Lewis comedies, for instance) which had been consigned to the cultural junk heap by critics and theorists alike.

Since American film was the chief beneficiary of the *auteur* theory, it is not surprising that it caught the imagination of American film scholars more than any previous approach. The controversy which it provoked peaked in the 1960s, and helped to build a stronger film culture in academe. Andrew Sarris (1962–3) complained about the lack of a decent intellectual context in which the auteurist debate could take place. As he saw it then, 'film scholarship remains largely an amateur undertaking' devoid of the 'most elementary academic tradition'. Auteurism was possibly a key factor in changing this situation, as it did help to usher in a tradition of director-dominated film teaching which was essentially modelled on literary studies – and it is not hard to see why.

Before following this trail further, a cautionary note. We are not dealing with a homogeneous body of theory here, nor does it cross national or ideological boundaries without modification. So the following summaries of its repercussions may appear a little contradictory. Nevertheless, they are contradictions we need to explore.

On the one hand, then, auteurist theories gave films authors and thus bound them even more closely into a literary/aesthetic mode of analysis. On the other hand, since Truffaut was using the American cinema as a club with which to beat his French antagonists, American films which had been dismissed as predictable and formulaic were recovered. Genre films in particular – westerns, musicals, thrillers, gangster films – were now deemed to be interesting. The range of material considered by film theorists thus widened, so that Hollywood movies were now accepted, but only so that they could be dealt with in oddly inappropriate ways. Discussions of the newly respectable Hollywood directors revolved around the construction of a 'canon' of their best works (a body of 'classical' works held to be the best of their kind and therefore worthy of study). This was a critical practice which precisely paralleled the dominant modes of literary criticism of the time, and it produced similar results – the canon of film greats which now decorate film courses around the world. Popular film was thus incorporated into an alien critical tradition.

Only further reading can fully uncover the complexities of the auteurist debate; suffice here to stress a number of important aspects of its influences on film studies. Firstly, in one of its manifestations, *auteur* film theory followed on from the interest in *mise-en-scène* to concentrate on visual style – on the way in which films were composed and constructed for the viewer. Many auteurist critics uncover a stylistic 'signature' in the visuals which they attribute to an author/*auteur*, and this has become a customary critical practice.

Another strand interested itself in film genres. 'Genre' is a term appropriated from literary studies and used to describe the way in which groups of narrative conventions (involving plot, character, and even locations or set design) become organized into recognizable types of narrative entertainment – westerns or musicals, for instance. Auteurist critics realized that these sets of conventions were used by audiences as well as film-makers. Therefore they must exercise some determining power over what a director could and could not do if, for instance, s/he wanted to make something which an audience would recognize as a western. The constraints of the genre limited the ways in which any authorial signature might be inscribed, let alone detected. The genre was also seen as a convention to be *challenged* by many directors. Inevitably, work had to be done on defining the genre in order to understand its variations.

Such work revealed how dynamic genres are, how they continually change, modulate, and redefine themselves; genre emerges as the product of a three-way negotiation between audiences, filmmakers, and film producers. This raised an issue which became prominent later: the role of the film as a commodity – a marketable product sold to an audience through, among other things, its genre. More significantly, these enquiries began a long series of revaluations of the notion of genre, the study of the relationships between audiences and movies, and a better understanding of the pleasure of the familiar and predictable in popular entertainment – partially qualifying the hitherto conventional privileging of the novel, the unique, and the original. Further discussion of this aspect will occur in Chapters 4 and 5.

Lastly, and in yet another configuration, some *auteur* theorists moved away from their grounding in literary/aesthetic modes of analysis entirely, and embraced those of linguistics, anthropology, and semiotics. This is an early clue to the future of film studies, which increasingly became a site for the application of theories developed in other disciplines. The common element between linguistics and anthropology was the group of theories under the umbrella term of structuralism. Structuralism accepts that films are produced by film-makers, but it also reminds us that film-makers are themselves 'produced' by the culture. So structuralist theory has been very useful in reconnecting film with the culture it represents. It has also offered ways of looking at film as a set of languages, a system for making meaning, and has thus furthered our understanding of what the medium is. We will talk more about this in later chapters.

THE INSTITUTIONALIZATION OF FILM STUDIES

Although writing about the movies has been a familiar aspect of popular culture since the beginning of this century, it is only relatively recently that journals and magazines which deal with film on an academic level have become established. Even in the 1960s, many influential articles were published in journals which were not devoted to film at all; Sarris wrote much of his auteurist criticism in *The Village Voice*, while the *New Left Review* was a location for much screen criticism in the UK. In Australia, much of the agitation for the support of the film industry had to go on through the mainstream press, the newspapers, and magazines such as *Nation*. Predictably, growth in film scholarship and publishing accompanies the gradual encroachment of academic institutions upon the study of film and ultimately into teaching its practices too. *Star Wars'* director, George Lucas, is a sign of the times – a graduate of a film school, not the product of an industry.

The typical film department to emerge out of the expansion of the 1960s and 1970s is easily characterized: it is American, an offshoot of an English literature department, dominated by young staff with an auteurist outlook who prefer European films to Hollywood films. On its courses would be a few Hollywood directors: John Ford and Alfred Hitchcock might share the semester with Eisenstein, Fritz Lang, and the European modernists. The characterization is not without some validity. Film departments grew out of recognized disciplines which already had an established aesthetic viewpoint which fitted well with auteurism. The modernism of much contemporary European film – its symbolism, its reflectiveness, its overall literariness – enabled such departments to treat films as literature with pictures. It was a method of analysis and an institutionalization that is still in the process of transformation.

It has been argued that the late 1960s offered slightly more adventurous fare for mainstream cinema, tapping a younger, more visually literate audience (the 'TV generation') whose assumptions about film were not literary/aesthetic at all. Films such as *Bonnie and Clyde* (1967) or *The Graduate* (1968) demanded a relatively sophisticated audience, and got it despite the critics (who hated *Bonnie and Clyde*). It is true that this period sees some rejuvenation of interest in feature films at a number of levels and although it does not produce dramatic changes in the box-office, apart from the freak boom year of 1968, a wider film culture of some variety and sophistication gradually came into being. (The growth of the art-house and specialized cinemas discussed in Chapter 1 is implicated in this development.) This has affected academic study of film. Bill Nichols wrote in 1974 that 'whereas no more than a few years ago' film journals tended not to deal with theory at all, at the time of writing '*Film Quarterly*, *Film Comment*, *Cinema*, *Women and Film*, *December*, *The Velvet Light Trap*, and *Jump Cut* have published an appreciable body of formal criticism, joining the English magazine *Screen* and the French journals *Cahiers du Cinéma* and *Cinéthique*' (Nichols 1976: 7). The revival of Australian cinema coincided with the growth of a new audience, a new awareness of film as cultural capital and the importance of a popular cinema, and the launching of such journals as *Cinema Papers* and the *Australian Journal of Screen Theory*. It could be argued that it was in such ventures rather than in the academic institutions that film culture was most dynamic. From the new journals a reorientation of film studies could be abstracted; they presented a view of film as a means of communication, a set of languages, a system of signification – not just the seventh art.

FILM AS SOCIAL PRACTICE

The key to this change of approach has already been mentioned: the insertion into film studies of methods taken from other disciplines, including linguistics, psychoanalysis, anthropology, and semiotics. Some of these 'disciplines' were themselves hybrids, already crossing traditional disciplinary boundaries. The structuralism used in Peter Wollen's work (1972) on genre, for instance, employs concepts from linguistics and anthropology which are ultimately aimed at understanding the nature of the human mind.

In such instances, film is not even the final target of enquiry, but part of a wider argument about *representation* – the social process of making images, sounds, signs, stand for something – in film or television. Odd as this might sound, what emerges is a body of approaches to film that is rich when applied to film but which is not confined to the analysis of film. In effect, film theory becomes part of the wider field of disciplines and approaches called cultural studies.

The cultural studies influence on film theory was not particularly direct at first. Cultural studies initially analysed the ways by which social meanings are generated through culture – a society's way of life and system of values as revealed through such apparently ephemeral forms and practices as television, radio, sports, comics, film, music, and fashion. The influence of a variety of British interventions – the establishment of the Centre for Contemporary Cultural Studies at Birmingham or the popular culture course at the Open University – and the support of French theorists such as

Barthes and Althusser, generated research into the function, practices, and processes of culture. 'Culture' came to be redefined as the processes which construct a society's way of life: its systems for producing meaning, sense, or consciousness, especially those systems and media of representation which give images their cultural significance. Film, TV, and advertising thus became prime targets for research and 'textual' analysis. Within this research, culture is seen to be composed of interconnected systems of meaning. So one might begin by examining comic strips and wind up talking about codes of dress within urban subcultures. Inevitably, film became involved in such discussions; if, for example, one was examining the ways in which a youth subculture defined itself – through fashion, for instance – the role of fan magazines, the music press, and television might become very important. To follow the function of the fan magazines one might also need to know about their subject matter – film, television, music. Accordingly, in order to understand better how film might be part of the cultural systems under analysis it became necessary to enquire more closely into film itself as a specific means of producing and reproducing cultural significance.

Some of these enquiries looked very familiar; for example, historical studies of the industry and its institutions. Other projects looked unlike anything that had come before, partly on account of the apparently oblique angle of approach. For example, research into TV became a major item on the cultural studies agenda. Rejecting American research which looked for behavioural evidence of TV's effect on its audiences, cultural studies approaches turned instead to the analysis of the TV message – 'reading' the audience's response from the specific sound and images on the screen. Clearly, there was potential for overlap between the methods used to do this and film analysis. TV analysis had borrowed some of its assumptions from film theory in the first place. Film journals broadened to include TV and theorists moved freely from one medium to the other. A publication outlet for many of the innovative materials being taught at the Open University was provided by its link with the British Film Institute. Film was examined as a cultural product and as a social practice, valuable both for itself and for what it could tell us of the systems and processes of culture. Ironically, this enclosure of film within the culture – a reduction of its importance as a practice in some ways –

has resulted in a greater understanding of its specificity as a medium.

Although film studies are established in institutions around the world, we are now at a crucial stage in their development. Film is revealed as not so much a separate discipline as a set of distinct social practices, a set of languages, and an industry. The current approaches to film come from a wide range of disciplines – linguistics, psychology, anthropology, literary criticism, and history – and serve a range of political positions – Marxism, feminism, and nationalism. But it has become clear that the reason we want to examine film at all is because it is a source of pleasure and significance for so many in our culture. The relations which make this possible – between the image and the viewer, the industry and the audience, narrative and culture, form and ideology – are the ones now isolated for examination by film studies, and by this book.

We can now begin to deal with some of the specifics. In the following chapter we start with the 'languages' film uses to produce significance and pleasure.

SUGGESTIONS FOR FURTHER WORK

1. This chapter offers a very brief overview. Many of the articles referred to and positions summarized in it can be found in collections of film theory, such as Bill Nichols's *Movies and Methods* (1976; 1985) or Mast and Cohen's *Film Theory and Criticism* (1985).
2. How much of a difference can you see between montage and *mise-en-scène*? Look at some television advertisements and see if you can: (a) isolate both styles of filming/editing, and (b) distinguish different effects pursued by both.
3. Examine the film reviews in your quality dailies or weeklies and see if you can determine their underlying theoretical assumptions. Is any one approach dominant? Why do you think this is so?
4. How convinced are you of the analogy drawn between English literature departments and film studies departments? What are its limits? Has the growth of communications or cultural studies programmes made any difference?
5. If possible, it is worth looking at the films which are used to support the various theoretical positions. For example, try

examining *The Battleship Potemkin* in order to understand the virtues of montage and expressive film-making; or look at *Metropolis* or *The Cabinet of Dr Caligari* for expressionist film-making; or, finally, examine a series of John Ford westerns to see how far the requirements of the genre and the personal qualities of a director can be separated.

6. The key movement we have examined is away from the film/reality relationship and towards the film/audience relationship. Do you see why that might be important? It is worth reading Brian Henderson's article (1971b) 'Two types of film theory' for what he has to say on this topic.

7. Further reading: John Caughie's *Theories of Authorship* (1981) is a collection of articles dealing with *auteur* theory and related issues. Australian readers can take advantage of Dugald Williamson's introduction of such theories, *Authorship and Criticism* (1986). A good example of cultural criticism of film and television, although not at an introductory level, is Bennett *et al.* (eds) *Popular Television and Film* (1981). For those who might want to examine more conventional introductions to film study, Bordwell and Thompson's *Film Art: an Introduction* (1986) or James Monaco's *How to Read a Film* (1981). A slightly more advanced introduction to film theory, with a British–European bias, is Lapsley and Westlake's *Film Theory: an Introduction* (1989).

Chapter 3

Film languages

The title of this chapter may require explanation. Film is not, of course, a language but it does generate its meanings through systems (cinematography, sound editing, and so on) which work like languages. To understand how this idea might help in our analysis of films, and to understand the limits of this idea, we need to go back to some very basic principles. The first step is to see film as communication. The second step is to place film communication within a wider system for generating meaning – that of the culture itself.

CULTURE AND LANGUAGE

Notoriously difficult to define neatly, culture, as I wish to discuss it here, is a dynamic process which produces the behaviours, the practices, the institutions, and the meanings which constitute our social existence. Culture comprises the processes of making sense of our way of life. Cultural studies theorists, drawing particularly on semiotics, have argued that language is the major mechanism through which culture produces and reproduces social meanings. The definition of language developed in this tradition of thought goes well beyond that of the normal definition of verbal or written language. For semioticians such as Roland Barthes (1973), 'language' includes all those systems from which we can select and combine elements in order to communicate. So dress can be a language; by changing our fashions (selecting and combining our garments and thus the meanings that culture attributes to them) we can change what our clothes 'say' about us and our place within the culture.

Ferdinand de Saussure is commonly held to be the founder of

European semiotics. He argued that language is not, as is commonly thought, a system of nomenclature. We do not simply invent names for things as they are encountered or invented; thus the Bible story of Adam naming the objects in Eden cannot be an accurate account of how language works (whatever else it might be). If language simply named things, there would be no difficulty in translating from one language to another. But there is difficulty, because cultures share some concepts and objects but not others. The Eskimos have many words for snow, since it has great significance within their physical and social worlds; Australian Aboriginal languages have no word for money as the function that money serves does not exist within their original cultures; and every viewer of westerns will know that American Indians were supposed to be unable to comprehend the concept of lying (i.e. their language did not enable them to 'think it' or 'talk it'): hence the formula 'white man speak with forked tongue'. Even cultures which share the same language are not made up of precisely the same components, and so Australians, Americans, and Britons will attribute significance to the components of their worlds in different ways. The language system of a culture carries that culture's system of priorities, its specific set of values, its specific composition of the physical and social world.

What language does is to construct, not label, reality for us. We cannot think without language, so it is difficult to imagine 'thinking' things for which we have no language. We become members of our culture through language, we acquire our sense of personal identity through language, and we internalize the value systems which structure our lives through language. We cannot step 'outside' language in order to produce a set of our own meanings which are totally independent of the cultural system.

Nevertheless, it is possible to use our language to say new things, to articulate new concepts, to incorporate new objects. But we do this through existing terms and meanings, through the existing vocabularies of words and ideas in our language. A new object might be defined by connecting it with existing analogous objects – as is clear in the word 'typewriter' – or new ideas will interpellate themselves by trying to redefine current terms and usage – as feminism has done in its attack on sexist usage. Individual utterances are thus both unique *and* culturally determined. This apparent contradiction is explained by Saussure's useful distinction between the *langue* of the culture (the potential for individual utterances within a language system), and the *parole* (the individual utterance composed by choices from the *langue*). The distinction roughly corresponds to that between language and speech, and it reminds us that, although there are vast possibilities for originality in the *langue*, there are also things we cannot say, meanings that cannot be produced within any one specific language system.

All of the above is as true of film 'languages' as it is of verbal language, although the connection to film may seem a little distant at the moment. The operation of language, however, provides us with a central model of the way culture produces meaning, regardless of the medium of communication.

Language constructs meanings in two ways. The literal or denotative meaning of a word is attached to it by usage. It is a dictionary style of meaning where the relation between the word and the object it refers to is relatively fixed. The word 'table' is widely understood to refer to a flat object on (usually) four legs upon which we might rest our dinner, books, or a vase, and which has variants such as the coffee table and the dinner table. The denotative meaning is not its only meaning (in fact, it is doubtful that anything is understood purely literally). Words, and the things to which they refer, accrue associations, connotations, and social meanings, as they are used. The word 'politician', for instance, is not a neutral word in most western cultures. It can be used as a term of abuse or criticism, or even as a sly compliment to someone who is not actually a politician but who manipulates people with sufficient subtlety to invite the comparison. The word can have specifically negative connotations because it can mobilize the negative associations attached to politicians. This second kind of meaning, the connotative, is interpretative and depends upon the user's cultural experience rather than on a dictionary. It is in connotation that we find the social dimension of language.

Images, as well as words, carry connotations. A filmed image of a man will have a denotative dimension – it will refer to the mental concept of 'man'. But images are culturally charged; the camera angle employed, his position within the frame, the use of lighting to highlight certain aspects, any effect achieved by colour, tinting, or processing, would all have the potential for social meaning. When we deal with images it is especially apparent that we are not only dealing with the object or the concept they represent, but we are also dealing with *the way in which they are represented*. There is a 'language' for visual representation, too, sets of codes and conventions used by the audience to make sense of what they see. Images reach us as already 'encoded' messages, already represented as meaningful in particular ways. One of the tasks of film analysis is to discover how this is done, both in particular films and in general.

We need to understand how this language-like system works. Methodologies which only deal with verbal or written language are not entirely appropriate. So it is useful to employ a system of analysis which began with verbal language but which has broadened out to include those other activities which produce social meaning. The work of all these activities is called signification – the making of significance – and the methodology is called semiotics. Once we understand the basic premises of semiotics we can apply them to the particular 'signifying practices' of film: the various media and technologies through which film's meanings are produced.

Semiotics sees social meaning as the product of the relationships constructed between 'signs'. The 'sign' is the basic unit of communication and it can be a photograph, a traffic signal, a word, a sound, an object, a smell, whatever the culture finds significant. In film, we could talk of the signature tune of the shark in *Jaws* or the face of Woody Allen as a sign. They signify, respectively, a particular version of 'shark-ness' (those meanings constructed around the shark in *Jaws*) and 'Woody Allen-ness' (again, the mental concepts and meanings, both from within and outside a specific film, which are constructed around Woody Allen). We can also talk of the way different signifying systems (sound, image) work to combine their signs into a more complicated message; the helicopter attack, musically accompanied by 'The Ride of the Valkyries', in *Apocalypse Now!* is such a case.

Theoretically, the sign can be broken down into two parts. The *signifier* is the physical form of the sign: the image, or word, or photograph. The *signified* is the mental concept referred to. Together they form the sign. A photographic image of a tree is a signifier. It becomes a sign when we connect it with its signified – the mental concept of what a tree is. The structure of the sign can be represented diagrammatically like this:

To extend this, let us refer back to our earlier example, of fashion as a language. When we change our garments to change our 'look', what we are doing is changing the signifiers through which we represent ourselves. We change our fashions (signifiers) to change what we mean to others (the signified). Our social identities are signs, too.

Signifiers carry connotations. Semiotics has enquired into advertising to show how the selection of signifiers with positive connotations (water-skiing, relaxing by a pool) is used to transpose these associations on to an accompanying advertised product, such as cigarettes. Signifieds, too, accrue social meanings. You will react to a picture of Mikhail Gorbachev in terms of opinions you already hold about his controversial political career. Such a picture mobilizes a second, less literal, chain of cultural meanings through the specific signifiers used, and the ideas we already have of Gorbachev himself.

It is this second level of meaning we will be most concerned with in this book, because it is where the work of signification takes place in film: in the organizing of representation to make a specific sense for a specific audience. Semiotics offers us access to such activity because it allows us to separate ideas from their representation (at least, theoretically) in order to see how our view of the world, or a film, is constructed. It does this by closely analysing a film (or a view of the world) as a 'text', a set of forms, relationships, and meanings. Those wishing to follow semiotic theory a little further can find a good introduction in Fiske (1982) but for the moment a definition of the three terms, signifier, signified, and sign, is all that is necessary to understand the following chapters' application of semiotics to film.

Film narratives have developed their own signifying systems. Film has its own 'codes', shorthand methods of establishing social or narrative meanings; and its own conventions – sets of rules which audiences agree to observe and which, for example, allow us to overlook the lack of realism in a typical musical sequence. (When a singer is accompanied by an orchestra, we do not expect to find it in the frame just because it is on the sound-track.) At the level of the signifier, film has developed a rich set of codes and conventions. When the camera moves to a close-up, this indicates strong emotion or crisis. At the end of love scenes we might see a slow fade, or a slow loss of focus, or a modest pan upwards from the lovers' bodies – all coy imitations of the audience averting their eyes but all signifying the continuation and completion of the act. The shot-reverse shot system is a convention for representing conversation. The use of music to signify emotion is conventional too, as there is no real reason why the orchestra should build up to a crescendo during a clinch. Slow-motion sequences are usually used to aestheticize – to make beautiful and instil significance into their subjects. Slow-motion death scenes were in vogue during the late 1960s and early 1970s in films such as *Bonnie and Clyde* and *The Wild Bunch*; the aim was not simply to glamorize death but to mythologize these particular deaths – injecting them with added significance and power. Slow-motion love scenes both aestheticize and eroticize.

Shot 1

Shot 2

The spatial relations are reversed in the successive shots, as if to 'extend the boundaries' of the frame to include both parties to the conversation. The alternation of shots tells us they are speaking to each other.

6   The shot-reverse shot system for representing conversation

Genres are composed from sets of narrative and representational conventions. To understand them, audiences must, in a sense, bring the set of rules with them into the cinema, in the form of the cultural knowledge of what a western or a musical is. The role of the audience in determining meaning cannot be overestimated.

FILM AS A SIGNIFYING PRACTICE

Film is not one discrete system of signification, as writing is. Film incorporates the separate technologies and discourses of the camera, lighting, editing, set design, and sound – all contributing to the meaning. Mary Tyler Moore's repressed domesticity in *Ordinary People* is represented through the signifiers of her heavily made-up face, the décor of the house, or the combination of visual and aural signs in the editing together of shots of her tightly clenched jaw and the chomping of the in-sink kitchen garbage disposal unit. No one system for producing meanings operates alone in film. Michael Keaton's performance as Batman is constructed through (at least) the portentous sound-track, the choice of camera angles (he is consistently shot from below, exaggerating his size and power), the spectacular art direction, and inter-relationships between all of these.

It is now time to qualify the analogy I have so far drawn between film and language. Written and spoken languages have a grammar, formally taught and recognized systems which determine the selection and combination of words into utterances, regulating the generation of meanings. There is no such system in film. Film has no equivalent to syntax – no ordering system which would determine how shots should be combined in sequence. Nor is there a parallel between the function of a single shot in a film and that of a word or sentence in written or verbal communication. A single shot can last minutes. In it, dialogue can be uttered, characters' movements and thus relationships can be manipulated, and a physical or historical setting outlined. This may be equivalent to a whole chapter in a novel.

If there is a grammar of film, it is minimal and it works like this. Firstly, each shot is related to those adjacent to it. As we watch a film we often defer our understanding of one shot until we see the next. When we see a character addressing another offscreen, our view of the significance of those words may have to wait until we see the following shot, depicting the person being addressed. Secondly, unlike the grammar of written language which is to a large degree explicitly culturally regulated, relationships between shots in a film have to be constructed through less stable sets of conventions. Much depends not only on the audience's 'competencies' (their experience of, or skill at, reading film), but also on the film-maker's ability to construct any relationships which are not governed by convention.

The construction of a relationship between shots can be the first moment in understanding a narrative film. But the process is not as simple as it sounds. Readers will remember that Chapter 2 dealt with a major theoretical argument about exactly how this process worked – through constructing relationships between shots (montage) or through constructing relationships within shots (*mise-en-scène*). We know that these are not mutually exclusive and that both kinds of relationships are constructed by film-makers and interpreted by audiences. Both terms occur later in this chapter, as we move to a survey of the basic signifying practices employed in film production.

THE SIGNIFYING SYSTEMS

The following survey will not be a full taxonomy (I do not talk about titles or special effects, for instance) but it will provide a basis for work now and further reading later.

The camera

Probably the most complex set of practices in film production involves the manipulation of the camera itself. The film stock used, the angle of the camera, the depth of its field of focus, the format of screen size (for example, Cinemascope or widescreen), movement, and framing all serve specific functions in particular films and all require some degree of explanation and attention.

Chapter 1 mentioned the different 'meanings' of colour and black and white film during the slow establishment of colour processing as the norm for feature film production. We can generalize from this to point out that different kinds of film stock with their differing chemical attributes and consequent visual effects are enclosed within different sets of conventions. Often black and white film stock is used to signify the past; it has been used to simulate the documentary in the Australian film *Newsfront* and to offer a nostalgic tribute to the past in Woody Allen's *Manhattan*. At the moment, black and white is sufficiently unusual to have some power as a special effect; music videos currently make great use of the process to give their texts a high fashion or avant-garde look. Film stock which is particularly fast – that is, it can shoot in conditions where there is little light – tends to be grainy or of poor definition (slightly blurred), and thus reminds us of newsreel or old documentary footage. Most films try not to look like this. The aim now is to capitalize on the vast superiority of film's clarity of definition when compared to that of domestic video tape or broadcast television. Developments in film stock have had a significant impact on cinema history. The celebrated *Citizen Kane* achieved revolutionary clarity and depth of field (the whole image, from the foreground to the far background, was sharply in focus) by pushing the film stock to its limit and by experimenting with lighting methods. The Australian revival of the 1970s was assisted by Kodak's development of a new film stock which produced sharp definition in the harsh sunlight as well as in deep shadow.

The positioning of the camera is possibly the most apparent of the practices and technologies which contribute to the making of a film. The use of overhead, helicopter or crane shots can turn film into a performance art, exhilarating in the perspectives it offers the audience. Much of the appeal of Ridley Scott's *Thelma and Louise* could be seen to come from the spectacular use of the camera. Less dramatic manipulation of camera angles also has an effect on the experience and meaning of a film. The camera can be directed either squarely or obliquely towards its subject, with rotation of the camera possible along its vertical axis (panning), its horizontal axis (tilting), or its transverse axis (rolling). If a camera is, as it were, looking down on its subject, its position is one of power. In *Citizen Kane*, a confrontation between Kane and his second wife Susan is played in a shot-reverse shot pattern which has Susan (or the camera) looking up to address Kane in one shot and Kane (or the camera) looking down to address Susan in the next shot. Susan is oppressed and diminished by the camera angle while Kane's stature is magnified. In this sequence, the manipulation of camera angles is the major means by which the audience is informed about the changing relationship between the two characters.

Camera angles can identify a shot with a character's point of view by taking a position which corresponds to that which we imagine the particular character would be occupying. We see what the character would be seeing. In *Edward Scissorhands*, Edward's struggle to get his peas on to his scissors and then to his mouth is shot as if the camera was his mouth. An extreme example of such a point-of-view shot is in Hitchcock's *Spellbound*, where the camera adopts the point of view of a character who is about to shoot himself; when the gun fires, the screen goes blank. Point-of-view shots are important for motivation and also for controlling aspects of the audience's identification with the characters. The fact that the audience is under pressure to 'see' from the point of view of the camera has been exploited in varied ways. In *Jaws*, we are given numerous shots of the victims from the underwater point of view of the shark. The confusion caused by our discomfort with this alignment, and our privileged knowledge of the shark's proximity to the victim, exacerbates the tension and the impression of impotence felt by the audience and enhances our sense of the vulnerability of the victims. The height of the camera and its distance from its subject can also have an effect on the meaning of a shot. A conventional means of narrative closure is to slowly pull the camera back so that the subject disappears into its surroundings. Mike Nicholl's *Working Girl* ends like this. This technique can enhance the ambiguity of emotional response, or invite the audience to project their own emotions on to the scene. It does this because it signifies the withdrawal of our close attention – the end of the narrative.

Panning the camera along the horizontal axis imitates the movement of the spectators' eyes as they survey the scene round them. Very often such a movement is connected with the point of view of a character. The prelude to the gunfight in a western is often a slow pan around the streets to check for hidden gunmen, or to register the cowardly townsfolk's withdrawal, as well as to prolong the suspense and maximize our sense of the hero's isolation and vulnerability.

Rolling the camera gives the illusion of the world, either actually or metaphorically, being tipped on its side. This is sometimes done as a point-of-view shot, to indicate that the character is falling, or drugged, or sick, or otherwise likely to see the world oddly. It is also used in stunt and special-effect photography and occasionally for comic effect. It can be extremely sinister and unsettling, as in the slight degree of roll in the initial sequences of *The Third Man* where the first pieces of the puzzle of Harry Lime are introduced, or during the dramatic confrontations between Alex and Dan in *Fatal Attraction*. Camera roll most clearly indicates a world out of kilter one way or another.

The apparent movement of the camera, as in a close-up, can be accomplished through the manipulation of particular telephoto lenses, or what is commonly called the zoom lens. The actual forward or lateral movement of the camera apparatus is referred to as tracking or dollying, and it is often used in action sequences or as a point-of-view shot – the gunfighter walking down the empty street, for instance. As a point-of-view shot it can be very effective in enhancing audience identification with a character's experiences. A chase scene through a city street shot in this way can have a physical effect; it reproduces many of the perceptual activities involved in the experience and is thus convincingly 'real'. Alterations in focus have a signifying function. Most films aim at a very deep field of focus in which everything from the foreground to the far background is clear and sharp. Variations from this can have specific objectives. A soft focus on a character or background may pursue a romantic or lyrical effect, such as that achieved in Bo Widerberg's *Elvira Madigan*. A halo around a star's face, created through the manipulation of focus or lighting, or by placing vaseline or gauze on the lens, gives an exaggeratedly glamorous and dreamlike effect. 'Rack' focus is used to direct the audience's attention from one character to another. This is accomplished by having one face in focus while the other is blurred, and using the switch in focus from one to the other for dramatic or symbolic effect.

The composition of images within the physical boundaries of the shot, the frame, requires close attention, and the function of the frame in either enclosing or opening out space around the images on the screen is also important. Figures and other elements can be moved around within the frame to great effect. As Charles Foster Kane moves towards Susan in their argument at Xanadu, his shadow falls over her, signifying domination. In another scene in *Citizen Kane*, Kane is defeated but the audience gradually apprehends the strength of his resistance as he moves from the background to the centre of the foreground, dominating those on either side of him. At times, the frame takes part in rather than simply containing, the narrative. In the opening sequence of *The Searchers*, the titles and credits give way to an apparently black screen over which appears the title, 'Texas, 1868'. Then the image changes as a door opens to reveal that the black screen was a dark interior, the homestead, and through its door we look out on to the desert. The juxtaposition of an image of the wilderness with the enclosed, domestic world of the homestead initiates a chain of contrasts which are thematically and structurally central to the film. The frame is used to symbolic effect in *The Chant of Jimmie*

7   The glamour shot: Cher, from *The Witches of Eastwick* (used with permission, still courtesy of Village Roadshow)

Blacksmith where a tableau of the half-caste Aboriginal boy eating his meal with his white mentor, a minister of religion, is serially framed by, first, one doorway, then another, and then by the image's frame. The effect is appropriately claustrophobic.

Lighting

It could be said that there are two main objectives to film lighting; the first is expressive – setting a mood, giving the film a 'look' (as in Zeffirelli's Titian-coloured *Taming of the Shrew* or Hugh Hudson's hazy *Chariots of Fire*), or contributing to narrative details such as character or motivation. In *The Searchers*, again, there is a moment when John Wayne's Ethan Edwards turns to the camera and reveals the degree of his obsessions; the shadow of his hat has obscured his face with the exception of one shaft of light reflecting from his eye. The effect is sinister and alarming. A whole film can be lit in an expressive way. The gloomy darkness of *Blade Runner* is an index of its moral and spiritual decay and the uncertainties which dog its plot line (which characters are the replicants?). The blue/grey of gleaming technology and electric light is the dominant tone, only alleviated by the sickly pink of flesh tones and the bright red of lipstick. When the hero and heroine escape into the open country the sudden rush of natural colours is important in overwhelming the audience's understandable scepticism about their future. This film owes a lot to expressionist films shot in black and white (such as *Metropolis*), as well as to the Sam Spade *films noir* of the 1940s where a similar chiaroscuro lighting was used as an index of hidden, dark motives at work within the characters. The mode has been picked up for use in more contemporary *films noir* such as *Body Heat* or *Basic Instinct*, as well as in such TV drama series as *Miami Vice*.

Realism is lighting's second objective. This is by far the most common and least apparent aim of film lighting. If it is successful, the figures are lit so naturally and unobtrusively that the audience do not notice lighting as a separate technology.

The basic equipment used to light sound stages or film sets includes a main light (the key light) which is usually set slightly to one side of the camera and directed at the figure to be lit; the fill lights, which remove the shadows caused by the key light and mould the figure being lit in order to add detail and realism; and the back light which defines the figure's outline and separates him

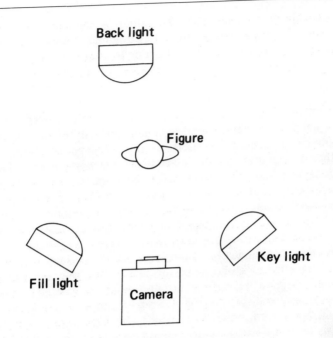

8 A conventional three point set-up for high-key lighting

or her from the background, thus enhancing the illusion of a three-dimensional image. In conventional high-key lighting, we view a brightly lit scene with few shadow areas, as the fill lights mop up any shadows left by the key light. Much expressive lighting, however, aims at exploiting shadows, and at lighting only part of the screen to give a sense of ambiguity or threat. This is called low-key lighting; it makes much less use of fill lights, and thus has sharp, deep shadows. Low-key lighting will often move the key light from its conventional position and move it to one side of the figure so that only half the face is visible, or increase the angle so that the face is lit from below and acquires a distorted, threatening aspect.

In general, high-key lighting is realist, while low-key lighting is expressive. These are conventions, which only work because we let them. But they are important constituents of the meaning of a shot and in many cases of an entire film. It is worth noting how lighting picks out and emphasizes elements within the frame, and how this appears to be a natural means of directing the audience's attention to one feature of the frame while obscuring others. This is particularly so during long takes, where a character can move in and out of shadow, into dominant or dominated positions, simply by moving from one regime of lighting to another.

Sound

Surprisingly little attention is given to the role of sound in the cinema. Dialogue can seem less important than the image, and in many cases seems to be used to 'fix' the meaning of the image rather than to motivate the image itself. Yet sound is important. It can serve a narrative function (as does the tune played by the spaceship in *Close Encounters of the Third Kind*); it is the basis of the musical; and it can provide powerful emotional accompaniment to a film's high points. Most importantly, if most obviously, it enhances realism by reproducing the sounds one would normally associate with the actions and events depicted visually. Music was the first form of sound to be introduced into the cinema, rather than a 'diegetic' use (that is, use of sounds motivated by actions or events contained within the narrative) although this is the most basic application now. We expect to hear the sound of breaking glass when we see a window smash on screen and we expect the words uttered by the actors to synchronize with the movement of their lips. The illusion of realism is dependent upon the diegetic use of sound.

Sound has other functions, too. It can be used as a transitional device. *Citizen Kane* often concludes a speech begun in one scene after the visuals have taken us on to the following scene. The overlapping sound binds what is an episodic and disjointed narrative together. David Lean has used sound cleverly to accomplish the transition from one location to the next; in *A Passage to India* he uses the sound of a medical instrument being thrown into a steel bowl as the cue for a cut to the coupling of two train carriages. The sounds of the clashing metal bind together as one sound which welds the two shots together. Music plays an increasingly important role in sound-tracks today. It can be used as part of the construction of the world of the film, as a source of atmosphere, or as a reference point to the subcultures in the teen films of John Hughes or the more adult fare of *The Big Chill*. Unlike the realist, diegetic use of sound however, music in films is usually non-realistic in that we rarely see its source in the frame or even within the world of the film.

Simon Frith (1986: 65) argues that the reality music 'describes/ refers to is a different sort of reality than that described/referred to by visual images'. He says music amplifies the mood or atmosphere and also tries to convey the 'emotional significance' of a scene: the 'true "real" feelings of the characters involved in it'. He calls this the 'emotional reality' of film music, and its aim is to deepen the sense of the film's realism, to give it an emotional texture otherwise lacking. It is this kind of contribution that Ry Cooder's music makes to *Paris, Texas*, for instance. Further, Frith sees film music as assisting in the construction of the reality of time and place, the world of the film. He uses the example of the music in *Zorba the Greek*, which is responsible for much of that film's successful construction of 'Greekness'.

A further aspect of music's signifying function within film is as much a part of popular music as of film. The cultural background audiences bring to films like *Wayne's World*, *Purple Rain*, or *Pump up the Volume* is crucial to their idea of what they see and hear. That cultural background specifies a range of musical, as well as cinematic, events. In these days of Dolby stereo and music-packed sound-tracks, music plays an important function in pulling the major segment of the audience, teenagers, into the cinema in the first place. The close relationship between the world of the music video clip (so often resembling a feature film on fast-forward in its rapid montage of narrative images) and that of the teen movie is evidence of how much of the same cultural space is occupied by music and film.

Theme songs offered at crucial moments can dominate the competition between signifying systems. The end of *An Officer and a Gentleman*, otherwise a curiously ambiguous film, derives much of its strength from the song 'Lift Us Up Where We Belong'. The nostalgia that permeates *The Big Chill* is saved from becoming cloying and sentimental by the continuous vitality of the music track. Certain instruments, too, become temporarily identified with particular effects; the synthesizer sound-track enhances the strangeness of *Blade Runner* and the same technique is used in TV's *Miami Vice*.

Frith's final point is probably his most important. Music and images have a lot in common as media of communication; they are not understood in a direct, linear way by the audience, but irrationally, emotionally, individually. Lévi-Strauss (1966) says that the meaning of music cannot be determined by those playing it, only by those listening to it. Barthes (1977) notes that it is impossible to describe music without adjectives – that is, it must be understood in terms of its subjective effect rather than through a dictionary of meanings. Correspondingly, its effect can be profoundly personal. Film music, like the image, can have physical effects: it sends shivers down the spine or makes one tap one's feet. It has been said that film music 'feels for us', by telling us when a powerful moment is happening and indicating just what we should feel about it through the mood of the music. Simon Frith describes this phenomenon more accurately and less contemptuously:

> one function of film music is to reveal our emotions as *the audience*. . . . Film scores are thus important in representing *community* (via martial or nationalistic music, for example) in both film and audience. The important point here is that as spectators we are drawn to identify not with the film characters themselves but with their emotions, which are signalled preeminently by music which can offer us emotional experience *directly*. Music is central to the way in which the pleasure of cinema is simultaneously individualised and shared.
>
> (Frith 1986: 68–9)

So the convention of music swelling at the point of a clinch is not manipulation but recourse to even more direct means of communicating with the audience.

Mise-en-scène

Among the confusing aspects of film theory is the use of *mise-en-scène* as a term to describe a theory about film grammar, a shooting and production style, and – as in this section – a shorthand term for 'everything that is in the frame' of a shot. We have already talked about the way in which camera contributes to the *mise-en-scène*. In this section I want to emphasize the importance of those other aspects of the image: set design, costumes, the arrangement and movement of figures, the spatial relations (who is obscured, who looks dominant, and so on), and the placement of objects which have become important within the narrative (the murderer's gun, the secret letter, the reflection in the mirror).

We learn much, unconsciously, from the *mise-en-scène*. When we recognize the interior of a dwelling as middle-class, bookish, and slightly old-fashioned, we are reading the signs of the décor in order to give them a set of social meanings. The film's construction of a social world is authenticated through the details of the *mise-en-scène*. Further, the narrative is advanced through the arrangement of elements within the frame; characters can reveal themselves to us without revealing themselves to other characters, and thus complicate and develop the story. The practice of watching a murder thriller involves the scanning of the frame to pick up the clues in the *mise-en-scène*. *Psycho* exploits this by offering us red herrings in the form of point-of-view shots which suggest that Norman's mother is still alive.

In films of epic proportions such as *Gandhi*, the plethora of information contained within the frame can itself be spectacular. The *mise-en-scène* in such cases is not necessarily narratively significant, but is rather a performance of cinema, a celebration of its ability to trap so much of the world in its frame. The funeral sequence at the beginning of *Gandhi* includes overhead shots of an enormous crowd. These shots display themselves, celebrating the scale of the images, the density of their detail, the impossibility of comprehending them during their time on the screen. Many historical films work like this, using their *mise-en-scène* to celebrate the power of the medium to recreate the real so overwhelmingly and thus, presumably, so authentically.

This is a large topic and one in which there are many subdivisions. Yet it is probably better to discuss the importance of *mise-en-scène* through an example, and I will do this in Chapter 7 in a discussion of the opening sequences of *Butch Cassidy and the Sundance Kid*.

Chapter 5 includes a discussion of the signifying function of the star but it would be remiss not to mention it here. The star has a function outside a particular film which is only partly incorporated into that film. Actors do not just represent characters, becoming invisible themselves. Rather, characters become visible through actors and it is always important to understand those specific meanings of individual performers which become part of the characterization. Stars can be sufficiently meaningful as to require the bare minimum of 'character' in the narrative; they are watched for their own sake, not for their representation of a scripted character. Although it is less the case now, the bodies of particular female stars were important drawcards for male audiences. Few went to see Marilyn Monroe films for her characterizations; few now see Bo Derek for hers, either. Stars such as Monroe or Derek are less common now, as we tend to see a Meryl Streep or a Jane Fonda as 'character' actresses. However, the event of seeing *Sophie's Choice* is still the event of seeing Meryl Streep perform (that is, do what Meryl Streep does) rather than seeing Meryl Streep submerge herself. Finally, the star's face is part of the *mise-en-scène*. The spectacle of the face of a Marlon Brando, a Michelle Pfeiffer, or a Mel Gibson, is a cinematic event in itself, and one could be forgiven for thinking that characterization was only a pretext for bringing this spectacle to the screen.

Editing

Here we move back towards the realm of montage, the construction of the relationship between shots. We should not underestimate the importance of editing. The famous Kuleshov experiments present a powerful case for its centrality. These experiments juxtaposed a single shot of an actor with a plate of soup, then a woman in a coffin, and then a girl smiling. The audiences seeing the three sequences identified the actor's expression (which never changed) as hunger, sadness, and, affection, respectively. Despite this demonstration of its power, montage is not so widely used now. It occurs most frequently as a means of representing a mood – cuts to shots of the sea, mountains, or crowded city streets – or for narrative 'ellipsis' – where sections of the narrative need rapid summarizing rather than full dramatization. In some cases the two functions are combined. In *Butch Cassidy and the Sundance Kid*, the period between the gang's escape from the US and their arrival in South America is summarized in a series of stills depicting the group's enjoyment of the pleasures of New York City. This fills a gap in the narrative and evokes a carefree mood which is abruptly terminated by their arrival in primitive Bolivia.

As realism became the dominant mode of feature film production, editing was required to contribute to the illusion that the film was unfolding naturally, without the intervention of the filmmaker. Now editing is more or less invisible, seamlessly connecting shots so as to give the illusion of continuity of time and space. There are exceptions to this – action sequences, highly dramatic moments – but in general the craft of the editor in realist films is to remain invisible and knit the shots together according to realist aesthetics. The search for realism, in fact, has produced occasional avant-garde films which do not use editing at all; some of the late Andy Warhol's films eschewed editing in order to let the cameras record reality without any mediation. Some directors claim to 'edit in the camera', that is to shoot scenes sequentially and cut the action at the appropriate moment for the transition to the next shot. This is both difficult and unusual.

There are a multitude of editing techniques. We have already mentioned two major ones – the fade-out and the dissolve. There is also 'the wipe', in which one image replaces another preceded by a demarcation line moving across the screen. The most frequent method these days is the simple cut from one shot to the next. As with most simple techniques, it requires great skill to do this well. Various transition devices can be used or invented to soften the cut and make it less sudden or disorientating: overlapping sound from one shot to the next; the use of motivations in the first shot which take us to the next (such as an action shot where the viewer wants to see its conclusion). Most realist films avoid sudden cuts unless they are to be exploited for dramatic effect. A sudden cut produces surprise, horror, and disruption, so it tends to be saved for moments when such an effect is required. The shower sequence in *Psycho* derives its effectiveness from the fracturing and prolonging of the action – a nightmare effect produced by the rapid editing together of numerous angles of perspective on to the murder. Again, in *Psycho*, when the murderer–mother is about to be revealed, the camera tracks in on the back of her chair. When the chair is spun around, revealing her skeleton, a cut is made to a close-up of the skeleton's face. The sudden cut exacerbates the audience's shock.

There are many editing conventions which assist the film-makers and the audience to make sense of the film. I have already mentioned the shot-reverse shot convention. Other conventions include the use of short establishing shots above a new location to place the narrative within a physical context; and the observation of an imaginary line across the film set which the camera never crosses so that the viewer is given a consistent representation of the spatial relations between the actors and their surroundings (this is called the 180° rule). Skilful editors can use the timing of their cuts either to enhance the energy of the action, or to slow it down. Action sequences can take on greater drama and complexity if cuts occur within moments of high action; as a car is about to crash, for instance, we might go to several successive and separate views of the same moment. Alternatively, a cut in a moment of relative stasis can slow down action, retard the narrative, and open up ambiguities. A thoughtful character, considering his or her future, may be shot from several positions in order to expand the moment and instil significance into it.

The speed, pace, or rhythm of editing is important too. Documentary film tends to use fewer edits than narrative film, and social-realist films tend to imitate this in the pacing of their editing. Many feature films pursue an identifiable rhythm throughout their length, and single scenes can be dramatically affected by the pacing and rhythm of the editing. It is easy to demonstrate this through an example. In *Mad Max II* (*Road Warrior* in the US), there is a chase scene in which the hero, Max's, large tanker truck is pursued by the followers of the villain, Humungus. Max has a shotgun with two bullets and a passenger, the 'feral kid' – a wild, 10-year-old child. During a desperate battle with the arch-enemy Wes, who has climbed on to Max's truck, the shotgun bullets roll out of the broken windshield on to the bonnet. Although Wes is knocked off the truck and disappears, Max still needs those bullets. He sends the feral kid out on to the bonnet after them while the chase continues at high speed. The musical sound-track dies down to be replaced by the sound of the wind in the child's face, and a heartbeat. At regular but gradually accelerating intervals, there is a series of cuts from the bullets on the truck bonnet back to the child's face. Rhythmically we cut back and forth from the child to the bullets, from the child to the bullets, from the child to the . . . Wes's maniacal face appears over the front of the bonnet, screaming in full close-up, and the return cut to the feral kid has him screaming too: a terrifying moment. The surprise at Wes's appearance is all the greater for the expectations set up by the rhythmic alternations between the shots of the child and the bullets. The combination of the alteration in sound-track and the skill of the editor has achieved this dramatic effect.

This point is important. Film is a complex of systems of signification and its meanings are the product of the combination of these systems. The combination may be achieved through systems either complementing or conflicting with each other. No one system is responsible for the total effect of a film, and all the systems we have just been surveying possess, as we have seen, their own separate sets of conventions, their own ways of representing things.

READING THE FILM

The complexity of film production makes interpretation, the active reading of a film, essential. We need to, and inevitably do, scan the frame, hypothesize about the narrative development, speculate on its possible meanings, attempt to gain some mastery over the film as it unfolds. The active process of interpretation is essential to film analysis and to the pleasure that film offers.

But films are not autonomous cultural events. We understand films in terms of other films, their worlds in terms of our worlds. 'Intertextuality' is a term used to describe the way any one film text will be understood through our experience, or our awareness, of other film texts. The moment of heroism in *Silverado* when Emmet doffs his bandage and miraculously finds the strength to do battle once more is clearly parodying the suspension of realism in many previous westerns. To see *Silverado* without the knowledge which it assumes of western movie conventions would mean finding it silly and inexplicably unrealistic.

Films are also produced and seen within a social, cultural context that includes more than other film texts. Film serves a cultural function through its narratives that goes beyond the pleasure of story. To examine this we leave behind the problem of film languages, and approach film through the category of narrative. However, many of the points made in Chapter 7 derive from this account of signification in film, and will further demonstrate the processes surveyed in this chapter.

SUGGESTIONS FOR FURTHER WORK

1. This chapter does not present an exhaustive survey of the language-like activities which contribute to signification in film. Further reading should include some other introductory books on film theory and analysis which may give a more detailed account of these practices. Examples of such texts are Bordwell and Thompson's *Film Art: an Introduction* (1986), James Monaco's *How to Read a Film* (1981), and the Sobchacks' *An Introduction to Film* (1980). These are useful texts, but do not approach film in the social manner of this book. Further read-

ing in semiotics might be fruitful, too. A good introduction can be found in John Fiske's *Introduction to Communication Studies* (1982) and more advanced discussions occur in Terence Hawkes's *Structuralism and Semiotics* (1977).

2. It is essential for any account of film to be conversant with the basic production practices. Attempts to produce a film of one's own, no matter how primitive, or a visit to a local film production unit, no matter how humble, will be of great assistance to anyone interested in the medium. Try and organize this, individually or as a group.

3. Building on the idea that a film is made up of a number of contributing systems, examine a scene from a film of your choice and try to break it down into its constituents. Try to determine just what has been the contribution of each element. Then propose a change in *one* element – the lighting, for instance – and see how that might change the meaning generated.

4. Examine the work of one system within a film – editing, for example. Is there an observable pattern in it? Can you detect any principles behind it? What is the nature of its contribution to the film as a whole?

5. What other language-like activities can you think of besides those mentioned in the chapter (dress, gesture, the discourse of film)? Does rock music, for instance, have a set of languages too? How useful do you find this analogy of language in dealing with film as a communicative practice? What are the limits of the analogy?

6. A further concept worth examining is Barthes' definition of myth (1973). Cultural meanings cluster, so that one signifier can touch off a group of related mental concepts. The image of the Sydney Opera House touches off a rich repertoire of ideas of the nation current in Australian culture, as well as simply denoting the building itself. Barthes talks of such groups of signifieds as 'myths', not in the sense of their being untrue, but as culture's way of organizing and explaining itself. Myths, as Barthes sees them, are part of our language and are embedded in all representational systems. We will deal with them further in Chapter 6.

Chapter 4

Film narrative

THE UNIVERSALITY OF STORY

Feature films are narratives – they tell stories. Even films based on true events will fictionalize them in order to produce drama, to telescope time, to avoid being filled up with too many minor characters, or simply to be more entertaining. Films are usually summarized by their plots – in their first 'treatment' (or outline of the script idea), in the advance publicity, in the TV guide, in reviews, and in conversations. Films may differ from other kinds of narrative – literary fiction or television drama, for instance – in the medium used and the representational conventions. They do, however, share with literary fiction and television drama the basic structure and functions of narrative. Much work has been done by researchers in the field known as 'narratology' on exactly what constitutes the structures and functions of narrative. Their conclusions are of great use to students of the feature film.

Narratology is a large field of study. Those who have entered debates about the function and nature of narrative within primitive and modern industrialized societies include anthropologists such as Claude Lévi-Strauss, folklorists such as Vladimir Propp, semioticians such as Roland Barthes, and British cultural studies theorists such as Stuart Hall. The reason for the breadth of interest is narrative's universality. Some societies may have no equivalent to the novel, but all societies tell stories. Story-telling can take many forms – myths, legends, ballads, folk-tales, rituals, dance, histories, novels, jokes, drama – and can be seen to serve many apparently different social functions – from entertainment to religious instruction. It seems that story-telling is part of our cultural experience, inseparable from and intrinsic to it.

What is clear is that the world 'comes to us' in the shape of stories. From the earliest days of our childhood, our world is represented to us through stories told to us by our parents, read to us from books, reported to us by friends, overheard in conversations, shared among groups at school, circulated around the playground. This is not to say that all our stories *explain* the world. Rather, story provides us with an easy, unconscious, and involving way of constructing our world; narrative can be described as a means of 'making sense' of our social world, and sharing that 'sense' with others. Its universality underlines its intrinsic place in human communication.

Not only is narrative common to all cultures, but there is evidence that there are structural similarities between the tales, stories, and legends produced by different cultures. The narrative structure found in the folk-tales of one culture can recur in another, suggesting that there is something universal in the structure as well as in the function of narrative. Vladimir Propp (1975) analysed a group of Russian folk-tales in order to see if they shared common properties. What he found was that all of them, no matter how widely they differed in their surface details (characterization, setting, plots), shared certain important structural features. The most basic of these were the functions of various sets of characters and actions within the tales. First, he reduced the range of different characters to a maximum of eight character roles. These are not separate characters, since one character can occupy a number of roles or 'spheres of action' as Propp calls them and one role may be played by a number of different characters. They are:

1. the villain
2. the donor (provider)
3. the helper
4. the princess (or sought-for person) and her father
5. the dispatcher
6. the hero or victim
7. the false hero.

All characters or 'spheres of action' which occur in folk-tales are accommodated by this list. This group of characters then participates in the limited set of narrative units or functions which make up the tale. From his analyses, Propp concludes that:

1. Functions of characters serve as stable, constant elements in a tale, independent of how and by whom they are fulfilled. They constitute the fundamental components of a tale.
2. The number of functions known to the fairy-tale is limited.
3. The sequence of functions is always identical.
4. All fairy-tales are of one type in regard to their structure.

We might understand the implications of this if we follow it a little further, into the basic structure he proposed for all fairy-tales. Propp outlined a list of thirty-one functions, themselves organized in broader narrative groups indicating their place in the development of the plot:

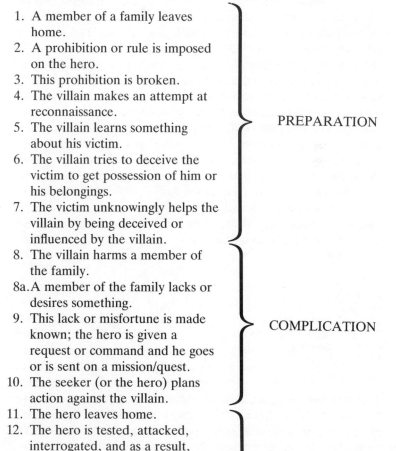

1. A member of a family leaves home.
2. A prohibition or rule is imposed on the hero.
3. This prohibition is broken.
4. The villain makes an attempt at reconnaissance.
5. The villain learns something about his victim.
6. The villain tries to deceive the victim to get possession of him or his belongings.
7. The victim unknowingly helps the villain by being deceived or influenced by the villain.

PREPARATION

8. The villain harms a member of the family.
8a. A member of the family lacks or desires something.
9. This lack or misfortune is made known; the hero is given a request or command and he goes or is sent on a mission/quest.
10. The seeker (or the hero) plans action against the villain.

COMPLICATION

11. The hero leaves home.
12. The hero is tested, attacked, interrogated, and as a result,

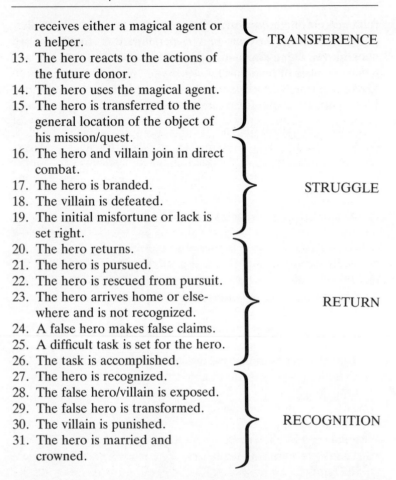

receives either a magical agent or a helper. } TRANSFERENCE
13. The hero reacts to the actions of the future donor.
14. The hero uses the magical agent.
15. The hero is transferred to the general location of the object of his mission/quest.
16. The hero and villain join in direct combat.
17. The hero is branded. } STRUGGLE
18. The villain is defeated.
19. The initial misfortune or lack is set right.
20. The hero returns.
21. The hero is pursued.
22. The hero is rescued from pursuit.
23. The hero arrives home or elsewhere and is not recognized. } RETURN
24. A false hero makes false claims.
25. A difficult task is set for the hero.
26. The task is accomplished.
27. The hero is recognized.
28. The false hero/villain is exposed.
29. The false hero is transformed.
30. The villain is punished. } RECOGNITION
31. The hero is married and crowned.

Not all stories will have all of these functions. But they *will* be composed from this list, and *only* from this list. Furthermore, they will all follow the order outlined. In some cases, sequences might be repeated – as in the struggle unit. The story outline is probably recognizable. The stereotyped cartoon plot involving the moustachioed, foreclosing landlord, the widowed mother, and the heroic son is apparent in the first seven functions, for instance.

While there has been argument about the comprehensiveness of Propp's 'morphology' of the elements of folk-tales, his work has been extremely influential. In particular, there have been numerous applications of Propp's specific conclusions (and his more general idea of uncovering a 'grammar', or set of compositional rules, of narrative construction) to areas other than folk-tales. Although there is a limit to the parallels that can be drawn between the cultural productions of primitive folk cultures and modern post-industrial cultures, Propp's work has been applied to mass-produced narratives in contemporary western cultures. Much popular film and television can be found to be structured according to Propp's principles. There have been a number of morphological analyses of films – for example, of *Sunset Boulevard* by Patricia Erens (1977) and of *North by North-West* by Peter Wollen (1976) – as well as more general discussions of Propp and the feature film (Fell 1977). John Fiske (1987b) has looked at programmes such as *The Bionic Woman* and *The A-Team* and found an extraordinary degree of correlation between Propp's functions and the narrative structure of the television series. We can easily demonstrate a degree of fit between Propp's categories of 'spheres of action' and characterization in film, too. A list of the main characters in *Star Wars* fits Propp's eight spheres of action quite neatly:

The villain	Darth Vader
The donor	Obe Kenobe
The helper	Han Solo
The princess	Princess Leah
The dispatcher	R2 D2
The hero	Luke Skywalker
The false hero	Darth Vader

We need not make too much of this as a way of understanding *Star Wars*, although it might flesh out vague claims about the film's fairy-tale, fable-like quality. It does suggest, however, how applicable to film studies much of the work on the cultural function and structural characteristics of narrative could be. At the very least, it underlines the possibility that the modern feature film and the primitive fairy-tale serve similar functions for their respective audiences. It is to the function of narrative that we turn next.

THE FUNCTION OF NARRATIVE

The fact that narrative is universal should alert us to at least two possibilities. The first is that narrative might be a property of the human mind, like language; the second is that narrative might serve an essential social function which makes it indispensable to human communities. At least one theorist, the anthropologist Claude Lévi-Strauss (1966), has attempted to relate the characteristics of myth and legend back to the perceptual mechanisms of the brain. So far, there is no way of proving or disproving such a proposition. It is, however, possible to examine the ways in which narrative might serve some social function. Lévi-Strauss, again, provides a useful starting-point here.

Lévi-Strauss (1955: 1966) examined the nature of myths and legends in ancient and primitive cultures. From them he believed he could unravel the structures of meaning and significance which differentiated one cultural system from another. Like Propp, he discerned common structures in myth which crossed cultural boundaries; however, he also saw a degree of cultural specificity in the particular transformation of these common structures. What all cultural myths, all primitive narratives, had in common was the function they served for the society. Myths, he argued, were used to deal with the contradictions in experience, to explain the apparently inexplicable, and to justify the inevitable. Within myths, contradictions and inequities which could not be resolved in the real world were resolved symbolically. The function of myth was to place those contradictions – between man and his natural environment, for instance, or between life and death – as part of natural existence. Myths negotiated a peace between men and women and their environment so that they could live in it without agonizing over its frustrations and cruelties.

So a body of mythology which attributes the vagaries of the weather to the particular dissatisfactions of a god (or gods) 'explains' those vagaries. The function of such a mythology is not necessarily to describe *accurately* our relation to a god or gods (although we cannot categorically rule that out either); rather, its essential function is to represent that relationship in such a way that those who have to can live within it. The notion mentioned earlier – that narrative makes sense of the world – is explicit in myth and ritual.

Lévi-Strauss suggests that a feature of mythologies is their dependence upon 'binary oppositions', a two-term conflict. One of the ways in which humans understand the world is through dividing it into sets of mutually exclusive categories – land and sea, man and woman, good and bad, us and them. These are binary oppositions and they divide up and thus structure our understanding of the world. They can do this because they are one way of determining meaning. Meaning is a product of the construction of differences and similarities; in this case, placing an object on one side of an opposition rather than on the other. This binary pattern is logically supported by the fact that we define things not only in terms of what they *are*, but also in terms of what they are *not*. 'Man' means 'not woman', 'not boy', and so on. We define things by aligning them with what they are like, and by separating them from what they are not like. Because this means we are placing things in already existing categories, already opposed to other categories, oppositions can 'breed', producing further transformations of the same binary principle.

In the following example we can see why feminist attacks on constructions of gender difference are so well-aimed. Assuming male and female are opposites means that, automatically, women *are* what men are *not*; if the male is strong, then the female must be weak, and on it goes:

male	female
strong	weak
rational	emotional
reliable	unreliable

With the gradual proliferation of items under these headings we can see the accretion of negatives on the female side as a necessary product of the assumption that male and female are opposites. To continue with the chain is to end up with good (male) versus bad (female). Ultimately, of course, all patterns of opposition – and thus their possibilities for meaning – are produced by large over-arching categories like 'nature' and 'culture'. (Men, for instance, in our culture are seen as physical, comfortable outdoors, and 'natural', while women are seen to be indoor creatures, emotional, and to be protected from nature. Men are 'nature', women are 'culture'.) Lévi-Strauss saw this perceptual and linguistic concept repeated in the structure and process of narrative itself, in its dependence on conflict and binary oppositions. Patterns of opposition can be traced quite easily through narrative and we will explore this notion a little more fully later on in this chapter.

STRUCTURALISM AND NARRATIVE

The theories we have been looking at so far fall into the general area of structuralist approaches. Structuralism has been very

powerful in its influence on narrative theory. Its main virtue is that
it is most interested in those things that narratives have in common, rather than in the distinctive characteristics of specific narratives. Structuralists look at films, for instance, to see how they fit
into or help to define a genre, style, or movement. As a result,
what they notice tends to be a component of all narrative, or the
narrative systems of a particular medium, rather than the features
of a particular narrative. This may be a weakness when looking
closely at one text, but for understanding the nature of the
medium of film it is very useful indeed.

What we can glean from structuralist approaches is an idea of
the way that narrative works. Of course, we already know that
narrative is set in train by the establishment of some kind of
conflict. Most films start by establishing the lines of conflict which
will determine or motivate the events and actions of the story.
Binary oppositions can be useful here because often the conflict is
between a pair of opposing forces which are mutually exclusive.
The hero is faced with a threat, a challenge, or a need which has to
be met or satisfied. Those forces which will inhibit the meeting of
the threat or challenge, or satisfaction of the need, are seen to be
in opposition (enemy-like) to the viewer who identifies with the
hero. So a simple binary system is set up in which we measure
good and bad through the determining category of the good hero.

More usually, however, we see the 'world' of the film as itself made
up of conflicting forces, loyalties, or value systems. The problem of the
film (and its hero) is to resolve or opt for one side of this opposition.
The conflict can be quite stark and uncompromising in, say, the
characteristic opposition between homesteaders and Indians in a
traditional western. This is how such an opposition looks (and note
how comprehensively this can structure the film in all its signifying
systems – the visual imagery surrounding the Indians, or the tendency
to emphasize the white's family but not the Indian's, for instance – and
note also how the basic set of oppositions breeds others):

homesteaders	Indians
white	red
Christian	pagan
domestic	savage
helpless	dangerous
weak	strong
clothed	naked

(Of course, this opposition, too, could be boiled down to a governing one – that of culture versus nature.) The opposition here cannot be resolved unless one or the other side withdraws or capitulates. The hero usually operates as someone who can understand both sides of the pattern: he is usually strong, not weak; dangerous, not helpless; and is often associated with the red man as well as the white. His role then is to mediate the opposition. In *The Searchers*, John Wayne's Ethan Edwards enacts vengeance on the Indians for the murder of his relatives (indices of his identification with the homesteaders' side of the oppositions) but with savagery, a lack of respect for the law, and (in the final act of scalping) a specific invocation of the Indian. By crossing the opposition, he 'resolves' it by killing his counterpart, Scar. We can see that the resolution is not one that could survive outside the narrative as a model for solving disputes, but that is narrative's function – to resolve *symbolically* what cannot be *actually* resolved.

In a different example the conflict is resolved by the main character repudiating one side of the opposition and opting for the alternative. The problem for Roberta (Rosanna Arquette) in *Desperately Seeking Susan* is that she has a fascination for something she is not, for Susan (Madonna). The conflict between her life and Susan's could be represented as follows:

Roberta	Susan
conventional	unconventional
bourgeois	anti-bourgeois
suburban	urban
married	unmarried
sexually submissive	sexually aggressive
boring	exciting
constrained	free

The conflict is localized in Roberta's relationship with her bathroom-spa salesman husband Gary. When she rejects him and his values in favour of a less secure but more exciting future, the opposition dissolves; it loses its ability to generate conflict. This film mounts an unusually strong attack on suburban marriage and will be the subject of a more detailed reading in Chapter 7.

The key idea here is that the oppositional conflict in narrative is not just a feature of narrative structure but is interwoven with the full range of meanings generated by the film as a whole. The binary structure produces not only the bald outline of a narrative but its specific images too; we see the specific opposition motivating key images in the film – Ethan framed between the desert and the homestead in *The Searchers*, Roberta in Susan's pyramid jacket in *Desperately Seeking Susan*. A pattern of opposition, once set up, produces both structure and discourse – the movement of the plot and the specific means of its representation in sound and image.

Another way of explaining the structure of narrative is to look at it as a process. Todorov (1977) sees narrative beginning in a stable point of equilibrium, or what he calls a state of 'plenitude' – when things are satisfactory, peaceful, calm, or recognizably normal. This equilibrium or plenitude is then disrupted by some power or force which results in a state of disequilibrium. This state can only be resolved through the action of a force directed against the disrupting force. The result is the restoration of equilibrium or plenitude. But, and so we see that the process is not entirely circular, the second stable point is not entirely the same as the first. Conversely, in some films the equilibrium at the end may be achieved through the recognition that we cannot change or affect the power of the disrupting force at the beginning. In the differences between beginning and end, we have the movement of narrative. Even in films such as *Mad Max II* (*The Road Warrior*), where the hero ends up almost exactly where he began, the state of equilibrium is radically changed by his having served the group which escapes through his self-sacrifice.

Todorov's explanation is usefully simple. It is easy to chart, particularly since most films allow their disruptions to occur near the beginning. The opening of *Once upon a Time in the West* represents a family setting out a festive dinner in front of their homestead only to be slaughtered by a gang of outlaws before they can eat it. While the characters in *Alien 3* take some time to realize that the alien is amongst them, the audience has been aware of this almost from the beginning. *Jaws* opens with a group of teenagers having a party on the beach (the moment of plenitude); two leave for a moonlight swim, the girl throwing off her clothes as she leads the way. Almost as soon as she is in the water, we meet the opposing 'force' of the shark and she is attacked. The shark, and the commercial forces which collaborate in its disruption, continue to harass the community until opposed through the combination of Brody, Hooper, and Quint, and a variety of more or less useless machinery. The shark's eventual defeat is the product of chance, but the audience's relief helps to mask the fact that the attitudes which allowed swimmers on to the beaches, unwarned, still exist. The 'plenitude' restored is one that is marginally different in that the immediate threat (the shark) is gone and the police chief is vindicated, but its fragility is revealed by the promotional legend eventually employed in *Jaws II* – 'just when you thought it was safe to go back into the water. . .'.

Narrative process could be represented diagrammatically like this:

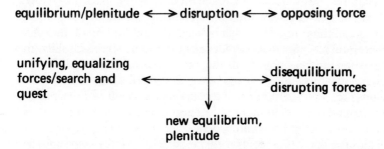

This process has an ideological dimension; that is, it carries a burden of social and cultural meanings which need analysis, and we will look at this in Chapter 6. For the moment, though, it is important simply to understand the fact that there is a common structural process in narrative which has a determining effect on what we see on cinema screens. Despite its immense variety and difference in forms, narrative is something we can describe. We need to consider now what differentiates one narrative from another.

CODES AND CONVENTIONS

When we want to deal with bodies of films, film movements, or even a single text, we need to look at the specific relations established between one film and the whole context in which it is viewed. This context will include other films as well as the full range of media constructions, advertising strategies, and so on that frame the particular film. This is ultimately a social context. The satisfaction an audience finds in a film does not emerge from the narrative alone. At the simplest level, film narratives are viewed within a context that is both textual and social. From the social context, connections can be implied between a film and social movements – *Rambo* and Reaganism, for example – or between a film and contemporary events – *Jaws* as a Watergate film, or *The Fly* as an AIDS allegory, for instance. As we shall see in Chapter 6, this can oversimplify the relationship between film and society.

For now, however, we need to be aware that the myths, beliefs, and practices preferred by a culture or group of cultures will find their way into those cultures' narratives where they can be reinforced, criticized, or simply reproduced. It is possible to apprehend social change through changes in thematic or formal trends in narrative over time. For example, in the nineteenth-century novel, narrative closure was often provided through the use of marriage as a mechanism which symbolized the education of the character(s) and the final achievement of their lives. Usually this marriage indicated that all the problems within the relationship were now solved. This was not a direct reflection of social attitudes, of course. Whatever the existential reality of marriage in Victorian times (and there are plenty of accounts which reveal that the novels did not accurately depict, let alone reflect, a social fact), ideologically it was central to the society. Today, our films are unlikely to use marriage as an uncomplicated mechanism for closure. In *Desperately Seeking Susan*, the abandonment of the marriage is presented for the same automatic approval from the audience as marriage once was. Roles identified with such actresses as Jill Clayburgh or Jane Fonda in films such as *An Unmarried Woman* or even *Nine to Five* represent marriage as a domestic trap which is limiting and boring, and even sexist. The meaning of marriage, and thus its ability to happily close off a narrative, has been altered by shifts in traditional attitudes to gender relations and in the ideologies which support them. Again, this change is not reflected by film in any simple way, nor is the change complete or irrevocable even now. Indeed, the career of such a film as *Thelma and Louise* reveals deep unease, in the audience and the producers, about the female behaviour the film depicts. *Thelma and Louise* is reputed to have been screened to a preview audience to test two alternative endings: the existing one, and a more optimistic version where Thelma and Louise escape. Apparently, the preview audiences opted for the 'harder' ending, where the women are emotionally supported by the freeze frame and the music track but narratively punished for their deeds by dying, presumably, on the floor of the Grand Canyon. Even this ending, however, provoked bitter critiques for its alleged advocacy of 'female violence towards men' (*not* something we encounter in many Hollywood movies!). Given such reactions, it is hard not to see the reception of the film as enclosed within contemporary ambiguities and uncertainties about the kinds of power available to women in our society.

With *Thelma and Louise*, the problem was not so much the idea of women 'striking back' one suspects, rather it was the way in which it was handled which offended some critics. This highlights the fact that the social dimension of film narrative is not found at the deep structural levels explored by Todorov, Propp, or Lévi-Strauss. Rather, it occurs at the level of discourse – the ways in which the story is told, inflected, *represented*. This discursive level is also the location of cultural specificity – where we can differentiate the dominant discourses of one culture from those of another.

This is not to launch us into the hunt for cultural specificity in mainstream film. But it does alert us to the social influence on film, an influence which is most active in establishing the sets of codes and conventions which make communication possible. At the most elementary level we understand the societies depicted in films through our experience of our own society. As we watch a film and understand it, we look at gestures, listen to accents, or scan a style of dress, in order to place characters within a particular class, taste group, or subculture, for instance. And if the gestures, accents, and styles are not those of our society we understand them through our experience of them in other films, or by way of constructing analogies between the film's society and our own. All of these 'clues' are codes – systems by which signs are organized and accepted within a culture.

The dominance of Hollywood and its corporate successors has meant that film does not always exploit cultural differences as actively as some other forms of narrative. There is a high degree of cross-cultural coding where audiences agree to accept an imported system of meaning for the purposes of enjoying the film. So if audiences accept the gung-ho invocation of America that they find in many American films – from John Wayne westerns to the *Lethal Weapon* series – this does not mean that they are being traitors to their own countries or necessarily accepting an American version of patriotism. It has become a way of coding the dominant filmic representation of certain definitions of duty, honour, and masculinity. An upper-class British accent linked with a certain style of dress and behaviour is coded to read 'comic Englishman' in many Hollywood films; in Britain, it is seen as an explicitly American view of the British. Even the coding of Hollywood, while accepted for the purposes of entertainment, will be subject to further definition and mediation by other cultures.

Narrative events can themselves become 'coded'; in film we accept that a knock on the head can cause amnesia, and that a further knock can cure it. Such cases exemplify an even more complex and conscious system of coding communication and representation: that of conventions. Conventions are like codes, systems which we all agree to use. 'Manners' are conventional – a system of constraints on and expectations of behaviour that is aimed at organizing social interaction to particular ends. In the cinema, we have learned to use a wide range of conventions which organize the film and which greatly assist the film-maker and his or her attempt to communicate. At the simplest level, it is conventional for us to accept ellipsis in film – the omission of non-essential parts of the story in order to avoid matching screen time with real time. So when a character gets into a car in one shot, and in the next has arrived at his or her destination, we understand that this is a convention, a shorthand method for getting a character from A to B without wasting screen time. It is conventional that films are only realistic within certain unspoken limits; they do not try to imitate the full complexity of life if this would hold up the narrative unnecessarily. For example, characters going somewhere by car in a big city can usually find somewhere to park immediately – something we know is highly unlikely but which we agree to accept in order to continue the narrative. No one really wants a twenty-minute sequence showing the hero looking for a parking space. When we talk of popular films as 'realistic', then, we do not necessarily mean they are like 'real life'; we mean that we have in a sense agreed to respond to their codes and conventions – their established systems of narration – as if they *were* like real life.

The clearest example of a conventional narrative system was established within classical Hollywood cinema (Bordwell 1985). Even now, within most mainstream Hollywood productions, audiences expect to encounter a plot centred around a main character played by a star; driven by a consistent set of cause and effect relationships; employing a double plot structure which links a heterosexual romance with another sphere of action (adventure, business, crime, for instance); and which uses the romantic clinch as the sign of narrative closure. Departures from such conventions within contemporary Hollywood cinema are usually seen as especially realistic and 'confronting' (*Silence of the Lambs*, *The Accused*), as especially 'arty' (*One from the Heart*), or as fantasy (*Beetlejuice*).

Conventions have built up around the representation of the female in films. Particularly in Hollywood film since the adoption of colour, the female is shot in a different way to her male counterpart. There is more emphasis on individual parts of the body, even to the extent of cropping out the head or face; more attention to the moulding produced by lighting; and a greater use of *mise-en-scène* for display. Hollywood film has turned the female form into a spectacle, an exhibit to be scanned and arguably possessed by the (male) viewer. Although the conventions of the 'halo' and the 'soft-focus' effects (achieved through veiling the camera or spreading vaseline on the lens) defy reality, they are widely accepted in representations of women. In films we are offered an impossible image of female beauty as the object of male (and even female) desire. This convention is no longer seen to be as 'natural' as it used to be. Laura Mulvey (1975) has argued that narrative film necessarily places all viewers (male and female) in the position of the male voyeur and that this is a direct result of narrative film's conventions rather than an incidental by-product. Certainly, the male body has never been displayed in the same ways as the female body or to the same degree. Although there are some changes observable in, say, the use of Brad Pitt's body in *Thelma and Louise* as an object of display and desire, it is still true that men are not usually employed as secondary characters who exist simply as spectacles of desire in the way that 'starlets' are used in a typical James Bond film for instance. Impossible images of femaleness can only exacerbate the already highly constructed view of women most western men pursue. Conventions of representing the female in film are examples of the dialectic action of film upon society in that the production of such images has made it more likely that further examples of such images will continue to be produced until the convention itself is overturned. This is an object of concern to feminists and increasingly to cultural studies, and rightly so.

The breaking down of such conventions relies upon audiences understanding that they are, in fact, conventions. That such an understanding is possible is an important reminder that all the parties involved – film-makers, audiences, critics – are very well aware of the working of conventions. Many films will themselves operate as a series of comments upon conventions – sometimes invoking a convention only to break it. In *Raiders of the Lost Ark* Indiana Jones is pursuing his abducted partner through a bazaar when he is suddenly confronted by a giant Arab wielding a scimitar. Up to this point, the film has shamelessly and self-consciously exploited every convention of the action adventure serial, milking every situation for its dramatic potential in order to offer as many 'thrills' as possible. In this scene, the Arab is grinning and chuckling in threat and challenge, and the crowd draws back in expectation of a battle. Similarly, the audience. We are given medium close-ups of the Arab and he is a convincing threat. When we cut to Indiana Jones he looks irritated, preoccupied; he pulls out his revolver, shoots the Arab in the most offhanded of ways, and then resumes his search. The expected battle turns to burlesque as the conventional expectations of a fair fight to the death are comically overturned.

Raiders of the Lost Ark, of course, manages to have it both ways; while it sends up the conventions of action adventure movies at particular moments, it also works within them for the bulk of its narrative. Working against the conventions which frame the representation of women in film, however, is not nearly so easy. As we have already seen in relation to *Thelma and Louise*, these conventions have their social origin in how women are generally seen and valued within the community. The social construction of the feminine rules out most of the possibilities we might suggest as avenues for changing the representational conventions in film. For women to take on more power within the narrative (that is, becoming the one who drives the action forward) is to risk being seen as masculinized – the so called 'phallic woman'. For women to resist acting as the object of male desire is also to reject most of the codes and conventions which structure them as attractive, sexual, beings. There are examples, however, of films which are talked about as attempting to resituate women within the Hollywood narrative system, and to change their meaning for male as well as female viewers. Sigourney Weaver's character in the *Alien* trilogy is seen as naturally powerful and commanding, without becoming masculinized or asexual. Linda Hamilton's performance in *Terminator 2* is also atypically powerful, although the narrative still forces her to rely on a man, or at least a cyborg, for her deliverance. Other examples, however, demonstrate how conservative ideologies of gender can be. The negative side to this new, narratively active, woman is apparent in films which see female power as desperately threatening: in *Fatal Attraction*, *The Hand that Rocks the Cradle*, and *Basic Instinct* the powerful, self-possessed woman is insane, obsessive, and needs to be destroyed. Despite such films, it is certainly the case now that there is at least a competing set of conventions at work which problematize the traditional representation of women in the cinema.

Within popular film generally, of course, it is never easy to challenge or disregard existing conventions. Popular films need their shorthand, their accustomed routes, to operate effectively. Once accomplished, however, the breaking of a convention can itself become conventional. *The Searchers* is a film which follows the search for a lost child kidnapped by Indians. A familiar plot line in westerns, it has a surprise twist in *The Searchers*. When the child is found she does not want to return. This break in convention has spawned a number of movies which are, as Stuart Byron (1979) has pointed out, precisely similar to *The Searchers* in structure and in the key fact that the object of rescue does not wish to be rescued. Such films as *Taxi Driver*, *Close Encounters of the Third Kind*, *Star Wars*, and *The Deer Hunter* all use this convention. Over the last few years action films which involve an all-powerful killer of some kind – an alien or a particularly demented murderer – have given their villains a 'second wind'. Typically, after the villain has been dramatically and bloodily 'killed', the camera moves off to (usually) the threatened couple who comfort each other with the knowledge that it is all over. But, of course, it is not. The villain – often made even more repulsive by their supposedly mortal wounds – returns for one last attack, a reprise performance of incremental mayhem, so that the hero or heroine must find yet another still more cataclysmic way to exterminate them properly. *Cape Fear*, *Terminator*, *Terminator 2*, *Predator*, *Dead Calm* and *Fatal Attraction* are just some of the films which come to mind. Rather than surprising us, this convention is now so familiar that we have built it into our expectations, deliciously waiting for the surprise attack we know must eventuate.

What we have been describing, then, is a dynamic system of conventions, rather than one that resists change. At its best, it works to give us a great deal of pleasure in our mastery of the

9 Linda Hamilton in *Terminator 2*: a sign of new constructions of female power? (courtesy Carolco)

conventions, and at its simplest it enables us to recognize what we see on the screen as pictures of reality. It is a system that makes possible the most interesting method of classifying films: that of genre, to which we turn next.

GENRE

One of the ways in which we distinguish between different kinds of film narratives is through genre. Borrowed from literary studies, where it is used to delineate the difference between satire and comedy, tragedy and farce, and so on, the term 'genre' has become a useful tool in film analysis. In film, genre is a system of codes, conventions, and visual styles which enables an audience to determine rapidly and with some complexity the kind of narrative they are viewing. Even the musical accompaniment to the titles can indicate to an audience whether the film fits into broad generic categories like comedy or western. Finer discriminations develop as the film continues, involving the recognition of a visual style perhaps, or a recognizable set of moral and ideological values which will be inscribed into such genres as detective thrillers.

What genre does is recognize that the audience watch any one film within a context of other films, both those they have personally seen and those they have heard about or seen represented in other media outlets. This aspect of genre, *intertextuality*, polices the boundaries of an audience's expectations. It can tell them what to expect or it can deliberately mislead them by offering expectations that are not going to be met. In general, the function of genre is to make films comprehensible and more or less familiar. Even where a genre is parodied or criticized this depends on the audience's recognition of and familiarity with the target. The choice of a black sheriff in *Blazing Saddles* is only comic if one is aware of how radical a departure this is from the conventions of the genre.

A genre often includes specific narrative expectations – recurrent settings, set-piece sequences of action (the shoot-out, the car chase) – so that the task of resolving the film's conflicts can be deferred on to the genre. The western's final confrontation between opposing forces is almost ritually represented as a shoot-out. Through the management of the shoot-out (who wins and how) the film-maker 'closes' the film. Generic conventions assist closure, confirming it as a textual force, and sharing some of the film's responsibility for articulating an individual resolution.

Genres depend on the audience's competencies and experience: on the skills they have developed in understanding films and the body of similar experiences they can draw upon. Although many films fail because they are too predictable and too much bound by the limits of the genre, many others fail because they are simply not comprehensible. Francis Ford Coppola's *One from the Heart* mixes genres as well as moving frequently between fantasy and reality; despite Coppola's enormous reputation as a director, the film irritated and confused its audiences who soon stopped coming. Films need to encourage expectations that they can satisfy; or if they fail to satisfy them there must be a plausible reason and a reward for the audience in the final denouement. A mystery thriller, for instance, will offer many possible resolutions to the problem it sets up as a way of misleading the audience until the appropriate moment to reveal the killer. Audiences accept this. *Psycho* deliberately and quite mischievously leads us to believe in the existence of Norman Bates's mother so that we will miss the real explanation of the murders. As long as this deception is revealed in a satisfying and convincing manner, the audience can forgive the deception. But a film which arbitrarily ushers in a solution without the support of a generic convention or without foreshadowing is in danger of offending and irritating audiences. Contemporary viewers of Fritz Lang's *Metropolis* usually react in this way to the contrived ending of the film.

It is easy to make genre sound like a deterministic threat to creativity. It is true that all popular media, not just film, have to deal with the familiar and the conventional more than do, say, painting or poetry. The individual perception is not given the privileged place in the popular arts that it is in more élite forms like literature. Instead, there is a pleasure in the familiar, in recognizing conventions, and relishing their repetition and restatement. Nevertheless, there is innovation and originality in genre films and the best examples can achieve a very complicated and delicate balance between the familiar and the original, repetition and innovation, predictability and unpredictability. Producers of popular film know that each genre film has to do two apparently conflicting things: to confirm the existing expectations of the audience and to alter them slightly. It is the variation from the convention, the innovation in how a familiar scenario is played,

10 Genres and stars: the key elements in movie posters

that offers the audience the pleasure of the recognition of the familiar, as well as the thrill of the new.

Genres, then, are dynamic. They change. Christian Metz (1975) has argued that genres go through a typical cycle of changes during their lifetime. In his view, the genre evolves through a classic stage, to self-conscious parody of the classics, to a period where films contest the proposition that they are part of the genre, and finally to a critique of the genre itself. It is a little early in the history of film to be certain of such propositions, but as we shall see later in this chapter, there is certainly evidence that such a genre as the western has evolved and exhibited the kind of dynamism we are discussing.

It is important to understand that genre is the product of at least three groups of forces: the industry and its production practices; the audience and their expectations and competencies; and the text in its contribution to the genre as a whole (see diagram).

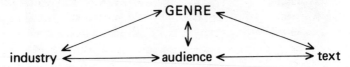

For the industry, there is often enormous market pressure to repeat successful versions of popular genres; hence the rash of sequels. Within the industry, films are often conceived in terms of genre, marketed through their associations with other films within the genre, and produced with an eye on the conventional limits of the genre. *Romancing the Stone* is a film which, in a sense, was made possible by *Raiders of the Lost Ark*, which itself allowed its audience to understand its genre by carefully referring to the serial adventure film throughout its length. Genre is one of the determinants of the audience's choice of a film, not only in terms of whether or not they possess the competencies to appreciate that genre, but in terms of what kind of film it is they want to see, and whether the specific example of that general kind of film (say, a comedy) suits their taste – is it a teen comedy like *House Party* or a zany adult comedy like *Housesitter*? Finally, the film itself indicates how it is to be understood through its own signifying systems by its intertextual links with other films.

Chapter 5 will discuss the specific roles of the audience in greater detail but it is worth suggesting here that audiences make genres as much as film-makers do. Also, genre can be as much of a challenge to directors as a restriction on them. While it may tend to restrict audience hypotheses about a film to the 'how' rather than the 'what', it enables complex narratives to be told in a minimum of screen time, actually enhancing the capacity of the medium to deal with complex and sophisticated material. Its familiarity, on the other hand, offers the many of us who want it the pleasure of seeing the predictable happen in unpredictable ways.

STRUCTURALISM, GENRE, AND THE WESTERN

This section will outline the work of one structuralist genre critic, Will Wright, on the evolution of the western genre. In his *Six Guns and Society* (1975), Wright examines the kind of cyclical development Metz argues is characteristic of film genres. He employs the combination of the methods of narrative analysis we have already met in this chapter: he uses the notion of myth associated with Lévi-Strauss, the use of oppositions as a means of describing narrative structure also developed by Lévi-Strauss, and describes a 'deep' narrative structure in the same terms as Vladimir Propp. In Wright's work – which is an illuminating but by no means flawless model – we can see in practice the various approaches outlined in this chapter.

First of all, Wright argues that the western genre in films goes through a thematic and approximately chronological change from what he calls the 'classic' western (*Shane* (1953), *Dodge City* (1930), *Canyon Passage* (1946), and *Duel in the Sun* (1947) are among his examples) to the 'transitional' western (*High Noon* (1952), *Broken Arrow* (1951)) and finally to the 'professional' western (*Rio Bravo* (1959), *The Professionals* (1966), *The Wild Bunch* (1969), and *Butch Cassidy and the Sundance Kid* (1970)). He acknowledges a further variation on the 'classic' western which he calls the 'vengeance' western and which includes films such as *Stagecoach* (1939) and *One Eyed Jacks* (1960). The way in which Wright charts this development of the genre is through an analysis of modulations in the 'deep' (i.e. as in Propp) structure of the plot on the one hand, and, on the other hand, the patterning of structural oppositions within the representational discourses of the particular films. There may be problems with his view of what constitutes 'deep' structure, but his analysis suggests both how we can detect movements in the genre and ultimately how we might relate these shifts to the social conditions which produced them.

Wright maintains that the western usually employs a set of four basic oppositions. It is through the ways in which the heroes and villains, say, are aligned around the basic oppositions that we can examine modulations in the genre and in the social meanings that they generate. These are the four pairs of oppositions:

inside society	outside society
civilization	wilderness
good	bad
strong	weak

In the classic plot the hero and society are finally aligned so that together they look like this:

hero–society	villains
good	bad
civilization	wilderness
strong	weak
inside society	outside society

As we move towards the more professional plot the hero is just as likely to be identified with the wilderness, and opposed to society:

hero	society
outside society	inside society
wilderness	civilization
strong	weak
good	bad

The change becomes clear through Wright's Proppian description of the narrative structure of each version of the western. The following is the outline of the narrative 'functions' of the classic western.

1. The hero enters a social group.
2. The hero is unknown to the society.
3. The hero is revealed to have an exceptional ability.
4. The society recognizes a difference between itself and the hero; the hero is given a special status.
5. The society does not completely accept the hero.
6. There is a conflict of interests between the villains and society.
7. The villains are stronger than the society; the society is weak.

8. There is a strong friendship or respect between the hero and the villains.
9. The villains threaten society.
10. The hero avoids involvement in the conflict.
11. The villains endanger a friend of the hero.
12. The hero fights the villains.
13. The hero defeats the villains.
14. The society is safe.
15. The society accepts the hero.
16. The hero loses or gives up his special status.

Strictly speaking, not all of these are 'functions' in the sense Propp uses the term ('the society is weak', for instance, is discursive as well as structural and is often simply a motivating device rather than a deep structural determinant). But we can see a clear outline of a plot in which the society is served by a strong individual and as a result absorbs that individual into itself. (This absorption can be extremely metaphorical and oblique, as in the relationship between the boy and the hero in *Shane*.) Society is seen as good, if weak, and the hero is seen as good and strong. The hero's capacity to live within society and accept its rules is one of the ways in which he is differentiated from the villains, so there is a strong invocation of social commitment and duty in this plot.

The vengeance variation has the hero initially leaving society in order to avenge a death or injury, usually that of a relative. Ultimately he is convinced by a representative of society, often a woman, to give up his quest and take up his membership in society again. In such westerns the plot has it both ways: the hero gives up his objective of vengeance only to find he is forced (by other factors) to fight and defeat the object of his vendetta. Here the society is shown in an ambiguous way; it is both weak in that its inability to punish the villain for the original crime is the justification for the hero's need for revenge, and strong in that its values are still sufficiently valid and powerful to convince the hero to uphold them at the end. The hero in such films is often depicted ambivalently too, as is John Wayne in *The Searchers* where he is both a servant of justice and a dangerous obsessive. Frequently such heroes prefer to live outside society – not as a critique of that society but as a signifier of their own implacable individuality.

In the 'transitional' western, the hero leaves society for more substantial reasons. He may be disgusted with its failure to support its own values which he may well represent, as a sheriff for instance. Society is seen as weak and hollow in *High Noon*, for example, and it was widely attacked as an anti-American film for its final image of the sheriff tossing his badge into the dust.

Finally, the professional plot completes the inversion of the pattern of oppositions found in the classic plot (in which, you may recall, the hero is eventually seen as good, inside society, committed to civilization, and strong). In the professional plot, the heroes can be seen as outside society; connected with the wilderness; and strong – although not strong enough to define their lives fully. They represent a critique of society, which is now placed on the bad side of the opposition. *The Wild Bunch* is a good example, as the outline of functions makes clear:

1. The heroes are professionals.
2. The heroes undertake a job.
3. The villains are very strong.
4. The society is ineffective, incapable of defending itself.
5. The job involves the heroes in a fight.
6. The heroes all have special abilities and a special status.
7. The heroes form a group for the job.
8. The heroes form a group and have respect, affection, and loyalty for each other.
9. The heroes fight the villains.
10. The heroes defeat the villains.
11. The heroes stay (or die) together.

Not all of these functions are entirely convincing, but the skeleton of the plot is caught accurately enough. What is created is an alternative image of society – the small group of professionals linked by skill and loyalty. In contrast to the classic western, the complicity between the individual and the society is broken down so that the heroes of professional westerns often find that the only resolution to their plight lies in a heroic and quixotic death defending their personal codes and reputations. Such is the way that *The Wild Bunch* and *Butch Cassidy and the Sundance Kid* end, for instance.

Wright goes on to explain this change at a number of levels, and readers may want to follow his account for themselves. For our purposes it is enough to point out that the political relationship between the individual and the society, or the hero and the values of his society, changes over time in this genre. Briefly, the changes represent society as inadequate, the heroes as more isolated, and all parties as less effective at resolving problems (death often resolves the narrative problem of heroes who are basically anti-social). There is an irresistible temptation to connect this shift in the markers of the genre with a point of view on an American social context, and the ideologies which construct it. Wright talks of large shifts in economic structures – the move to a corporate rather than entrepreneurial structure in business, for instance. Ideological shifts in popular culture which affect areas other than the role of big business in the post-war period (the role of women, blacks, western foreign policy, attitudes to socialism) would also seem to be necessary targets for analysis. The general view of society is much more critical, its value systems are seen as corrupt; so it is tempting to relate the changes in the genre to changes that also surface in reaction to Vietnam, materialism, and American foreign policy during the 1960s. One has at least to trace these changes in the audience and the industry, as well as in the texts.

Whatever the causes, Wright establishes that the genre shifts, and he takes us some way to understanding what the shift might mean. What he does, however, is largely at the level of macro-economic structures, or at the level of plot structure in the narratives themselves. He is less involved in the discursive aspects of particular texts and in fact depends on flattening out discursive differences to make his argument. This is a weakness which disregards the variety of film texts which can make up a genre. He also finds himself trapped into seeing each stage of the genre as exclusive of others; yet a film like *Silverado* incorporates all of the stages. And finally, this kind of genre study has to accept the role of the audience in influencing the direction of genres. So it is a useful test case, revealing the uses and limitations of narratology by reminding us that film narratives only exist in the minds of the audience. It is to these minds we turn next.

SUGGESTIONS FOR FURTHER WORK

1. Apply Propp's categories to a popular genre film and see how closely (or not) they fit. This might be used to introduce a discussion of just how closely one should draw the analogy between folk narratives and film narratives.
2. Look at the opening of a narrative feature film for, say, ten minutes and see if you can map the central patterns of oppo-

sition. Then compare this map with the final resolution at the end of the film. Does this process tell you much about the film's structure?

3. I mentioned plot conventions in this chapter – the blow on the head which causes amnesia, for instance. How many other such conventions can you name? If it is difficult to do this, it is because the conventions have become so effectively naturalized that we are unconscious of them.

4. Further reading: useful books on narrative theory include Seymour Chatman's *Story and Discourse* (1978) and Rimmon-Kenan's *Narrative Fiction* (1983); for further structuralist analyses, feminist analyses of the conventions of representation of the female in films, and genre theories, see Bill Nichols's *Movies and Methods*, vols 1 and 2 (1976; 1985). Constance Penley's *Feminism and Film Theory* (1988) is a good collection of feminist critiques, and David Bordwell's *Narration in the Fiction Film* (1985) provides an excellent account of the narrative system in classical Hollywood cinema. A useful and accessible account of genre theory and of specific genres is Thomas Schatz's *Hollywood Genres* (1981).

5. Examine a relatively contemporary western such as *Silverado* or *Young Guns* in order to see if Wright's argument still holds good or if there has been a further change in the genre's structures. A comparison between *Pale Rider* and *Shane* would uncover some interesting parallels and some direct intertextual references.

Chapter 5

Film audiences

It is customary for our society to see the media, generally, as a group of technologies which are unusually blatant in their devotion to the delivery of profits to the few through the exploitation of the many. 'No one ever went broke underestimating the taste of the public', as the cynical phrase goes, and this perception is most comprehensively applied to the major means of mass entertainment: film and television. In neither medium is it simply true that audiences are at the mercy of a knowing and cynical group of entrepreneurs who churn out the latest money-spinner in the easy assurance of inevitable success. Fortunes are still spent and lost in making movies. The top-grossing twenty movies in any one year will be the survivors of a field numbering in the hundreds – from American producers alone. Even those movies which we have come to recognize as classics are not guaranteed to make money (*Citizen Kane*, usually held to be an American classic, lost money at the box-office). Movies might be made by actors, directors, and producers, but they are ultimately made successful by audiences. Promotions of various kinds intervene in the process, but the way in which one film will catch an audience's imagination while another will not is a mystery to the industry, to audiences, and to theorists alike. Nevertheless, film is, as Christian Metz (1982: 92) put it, 'our product, the product of the society which consumes it'. It is impossible to talk about film as a social practice without talking about its audiences.

Admittedly, film audiences are not what they were. No longer is it the case that a family sees an average of one film a week, or that the same family finds most of the material available suitable for all ages. After the major decline in movie attendances that just preceded the spread of television in the late 1940s, a number of trends emerged which signalled a major shift in the constitution of the cinema audience. First, cinema audiences got younger. The majority of those who attend movies in the USA, the UK, and Australia (the three markets into which we have enquired) are between 12 and 24 years. (This age group seems not only to compose the majority of cinema-goers, but also to be a group for whom knowledge of the latest movies may well be of some social or subcultural importance.) Jowett and Linton (1980) have argued that the audience's level of education has risen, too, since the 1950s. This is probably predictable, given the spread of education since the war, but they suggest that the average cinema-goer in the US is now most often the bearer of a college education. They surmise that 'frequent movie-going is [in 1980] a much more élitist activity, as television absorbs the interest of those of lower education' (pp. 81–2). Cable and video recorders have complicated this (itself élitist) conclusion by now, particularly since the growth in the 12–24-year-old group of cinema-goers has accelerated markedly since their remarks were written.

It is possible to demonstrate, however, that there is now one age group which forms the potential 'mass' audience for films, together with a series of smaller segments of the market which require specific targeting to be called into the cinemas. Amongst teenagers, going to the cinema has retained something of its ritual status; among other groups this is less the case. In some segments of the market – the 'art-house' buffs, for instance – the ritual survives but almost because it explicitly *excludes* mainstream, 'mass'-market movies from its agenda. In general, audiences have developed very specific requirements of the films they choose and are unlikely to maintain a habit of going to the movies regardless of the title showing.

The relationship between the industry and its audience is sufficiently complex to make it impossible to determine precisely how changes in audience taste engender changes in production decisions – or the reverse. (As we saw in the discussion of genre in the preceding chapter, there are more than two variables to consider here.) However, the change in audience demographics – the concentration on the teenage and young adult groups, and the decline in overall attendances – has closely coincided with changes in the dominant genres of films being produced. The complete segmentation of the market, for instance, has made it very risky to continue to produce many films aimed at the increasingly mythical mass market – the 'lowest common denominator' so often invoked by critics of mass culture. Paradoxically, while the industry thinks of itself as commercially dependent on the big blockbusters, very few are actually made. Indeed, the 1990s have seen a trend, right across the mass media, of dispensing with the concept of selling to 'the masses' in favour of targeting specific interest or taste groups and satisfying their particular needs. Consequently, the 'family' movies and the big blockbusters are infrequent presences in our metropolitan cinemas, collecting around holiday periods and the peak seasons of summer and Christmas. (These vary according to which hemisphere one is in; Christmas is *the* peak period in Australia as it coincides with summer and the long school holiday.) Ironically enough, while the search for the blockbuster has made it harder for other kinds of films to get produced, the big successes have often been surprises – in the last couple of years we have seen *Home Alone*, *Ghost*, and *Pretty Woman* do exceptionally well at the box-office despite their relatively modest expectations. Consequently, it has become increasingly clear that the mainstay of the industry is in fact the smaller movie: in such films the genre is tightly defined, directed towards the audience for a particular star or director, or around a topical selling point – like Oliver Stone's *JFK*. This 'niche-marketing' approach used to sell the smaller films reflects some modification of production strategies. Over the last decade we have seen new sub-genres appear – the teen movie for one – and new *auteurs* whose reputations have become identified with these new sub-genres: John Hughes, before *Home Alone*, was best known as a director of teen films – *Pretty in Pink*, *Sixteen Candles*, *The Breakfast Club*, and *Ferris Bueller's Day Off*.

Exhibition practices, too, have followed the trend with multi-plexes which allow exhibitors to reach something approaching their former mass audience by placing spectators in different auditoriums each showing a different film. While it is true that the distributors' and exhibitors' level of risk and uncertainty has increased, and thus the conservatism of the industry seems to have become more pronounced, the multiplex does at least provide the material structure for a greater variety of films than existed previously. And although the impact of the video recorder was quite strong initially, the last five years have shown a steady trend back to the cinema, particularly in the age group that was a staple for the cinema in the early 1970s: the 24–40-year-olds. While video may supply narrative to its audiences, it does not offer them the event of cinema-going, nor does it replicate the experience of the darkened cinema with its larger-than-life images and Dolby stereo sound.

It is important to emphasize the fact that the nature of the event and the experience can vary. The audiences for *The Rocky Horror Picture Show* are now noted for turning up dressed in character, and participating in the screening/performance of the film by singing along, dancing in the aisles, or even climbing on to the stage in front of the screen. Some cinemas have taken the film on as a regular ritual, screening at midnight on Fridays to a devoted cult audience. Spectators not only participate in the narrative, but in its construction; they scream 'Cut', and 'Close-up', at the appropriate moments. At such occasions, film becomes, more obviously than usual, a performance medium. The ritual quality in film viewing is generally exposed when audiences see the same film repeatedly – a practice which is relatively common despite the theoretical assumptions that a film is made to be understood at one viewing. David Lynch's *Wild at Heart*, for instance, often turns up as a midnight screening for regular fans. For the return audience, the sense of power and familiarity is strong; no longer do they wait for the narrative to unfold but they confidently collaborate in its gradual development. This aspect of film – its ritual, performative quality – is often ignored but it is invoked every time someone says to us in a darkened cinema: 'Here it comes, watch this bit!'

SPECIFYING THE AUDIENCE

Contrary to popular wisdom, audiences are not gulled into attending films by distorting or misleading advertising campaigns. A phrase often used by producers refers to a film 'finding its audience' and this is a more accurate description of what actually happens. A film needs to specify its audience, not only in its text but also in its advertising campaign; in the series of interviews and promotional performances that may surround it; in the selection of exhibition venues (if there is a choice); even in the choice of the distribution company (again, if there is a choice). It is up to the producers and distributors to agree on the ways in which they wish to specify the audiences (or represent the film), and in many cases bad judgements are made. The Australian film, *The Chant of Jimmie Blacksmith*, was a sympathetic and thoughtful study of the plight of a half-caste in rural Australia, as well as a narrative

IT'S SHOCK, HORROR!

By TONY WRIGHT

THE queen of the cult movies, "The Rocky Horror Picture Show", will make a re-appearance in Albury on Sunday night.

The decidedly weird monster-musical has been around for years, but has retained a bizarre fascination.

The movie has been showing continuously in New York and London cinemas since its release six years ago.

Even in staid old Brisbane, "Rocky Horror" has been showing several times daily since July 1976.

The movie grew out of a stage show that became a cult after its debut in a dingy theatre in the low-rent area of Kings Rd, London.

"Rocky Horror" is a pop romp through a tasteless, tacky high-camp tale of transexuality set in a mad castle inhabited by Frank N. Furter, pictured.

It is spiced with catchy tunes and outrageous scenes.

But the most extraordinary thing about a visit to a cinema screening the movie is the audience.

The crowd tends to throw itself into the task of becoming part of the film.

With gay abandon, so to speak, true "Rocky Horror" freaks dress up in fishnet stockings and suspender belts, sing along with tunes, throw popcorn, yell advice to the characters on the screen, hiss the baddies, cheer the goodies and generally make whoopee.

The Albury Cinema Centre, which is screening "Rocky Horror" on Sunday night, could be in for a shock.

Weird rocky cult takes over city

11   *The Rocky Horror Picture Show* (courtesy of the *Border Morning Mail* (Albury, NSW))

around a true incident involving the mass murder of white settlers by three Aborigines. In the advertising campaign, emphasis was placed on the latter aspect – the logo featured an axe dripping blood – and links were thus constructed with horror films rather than with social-problem films. Already potentially marginal because of its racial subject, it did not 'find its audience' in Australia. Alternatively, the surprise success of *The Gods Must Be Crazy* in some countries seems to be related to its unassuming pattern of release (that is, the number, type, and location of cinemas screening it): it was allowed to 'sleep' for a while almost without promotion, until it built up 'good word of mouth'.

No amount of advertising will continue to pull people into a film they do not enjoy and cannot speak well of to their friends. The history of Hollywood is full of films which cost fortunes, which were expensively promoted, and which lost millions at the box-office. (*Dick Tracy* is a recent example.) Since the passing of 'classical' Hollywood cinema, and the decline of the movie audience, this risk is even greater. The disastrous *Heaven's Gate* is now a film which many have heard of simply because it was such a box-office disaster; few have ever seen it. Film producers experience great difficulty in predicting how audiences will react to each new production – and in convincing their backers to support any prediction they might eventually make. All they can do is try to specify as carefully as possible just whom this film is going to be for, and then try to ensure – through the release patterns and promotional campaigns – that this audience is reached.

Speaking of classical Hollywood cinema, John Ellis (1982) has said that there were two main ways in which its narrative images could be deployed to specify audiences: through the genre and through the stars. Although the audiences 'specified' are much more specific today, this is still largely the case. Audiences choose movies through their representations in the press and on television, and through conversations and other social contacts. These representations are understood in terms of genre, or stars where they are not already enclosed by genre. There is, perhaps, a third set of determinants: the broad cultural context in which the audience and the film are situated. The notion of genre was dealt with in the preceding chapter, so I will concentrate on the latter two categories here.

As suggested in the opening chapter, the context in which any film is released is constituted by a limitless number of components.

12 The publicity still: you will not see this in the film, but it advertises the stars, the setting, the genre, and in this case even the moral status of the characters is mimicked in their arrangement within the frame. This is from *Platoon* and depicts (from left to right) Willem Dafoe, Charlie Sheen, and Tom Berenger

There are the promotional and 'tied-in' productions – music videos, advertisements, hit songs, merchandise such as T-shirts, interviews, magazine stories, reviews, fan magazine items, and many more. In addition we might find that particular genres or particular stars have themselves cultural or subcultural status that is important. Attendance at a film can become a statement of membership of a subculture; certainly the cult around *The Rocky Horror Picture Show* supports this. Seeing rock music films often has the same significance. U2's audience will confirm their membership of the group by seeing *Rattle 'n' Hum*, and those of Prince's audience who were old enough by attending *Purple Rain*. The act of attendance itself becomes a signifier of commitment to the ritual of the fan.

Some films become newsworthy or topical at the time of release, often accidentally. Alan Parker's *Angel Heart* acquired useful pre-publicity on the basis of an explicit sex scene involving Lisa Bonet, the 18-year-old star of the wholesome American TV family sitcom *The Cosby Show*. (The example reveals how interwoven and comprehensive our cultural networks are.) As a result of the controversy, the film was at least initially constructed as 'explicit' (a small genre in itself) and had a recognizable name even before release. In another and more clearly unintended case, the coincidence of the release of *The China Syndrome* at the same time as the nuclear accident at Three Mile Island certainly had an effect on the fortunes of the film as well as on the residents of the contaminated area. In some cases, the context when the film is released is markedly different to that when it was made. A case in point is Susan Seidelman's casting of the singer Madonna in *Desperately Seeking Susan*. In the period between casting and release, from being a virtual unknown Madonna became an international star. On the one hand, this had the effect of specifying a large, possibly inappropriate audience – Madonna fans. On the other hand, it became very hard for this clever and interesting film not to be seen as an opportunistic star vehicle by some of its critics, or to be ignored by potential audiences who had a less than high regard for Madonna as a pop singer and, especially, as a politically regressive signifier of female sexuality. For what could be seen as a feminist film, this was a critical rather than a commercial problem. In a final example, Madonna's own *Truth or Dare* directly capitalized on her personal notoriety by claiming to document her on and off stage behaviour while on tour.

The cultural context can be a factor, then, in determining whether or not the film and its audience 'find' each other. However, overwhelmingly, most choices are determined by issues that are essentially generic (as we shall see in Chapter 7, even the problem with *Desperately Seeking Susan* was an argument about genre) or essentially to do with the role of the stars. It is to the cultural function of the star that we turn next.

STARS

It is unexceptional to make the point that film stars are implicated in the film-goers' choice of movie. However, the work of Richard Dyer and others on the 'meaning' of stars has deepened our understanding of just what this process involves. In his book *Stars* (1982), Dyer makes the point that the construction of a star's image within the culture incorporates representations of him or her across an enormous range of media and contexts; fan magazines as well as the mainstream press, television items and profiles as well as performances in films, conversations and hearsay as well as personal appearances. The importance of noting this is that the star in a film has a signifying function which may be separate or different from the written character within the film script. Stars are 'signs', not necessarily or entirely subsumed within the character they are asked to play. Since one can conceptualize a star's total image (as distinct from the particular character that he or she plays in a film), the casting of a particular actor has important repercussions on the effect the characterization will have. The casting of John Wayne, for example, was always determined by what *he* signified, the inscription of a particular version of Americanism. His later roles (in *The Shootist* or *True Grit*) were self-reflexive in that they commented upon this signifying function by parodying it or self-consciously mythologizing it. (Interestingly, it was only at this point that he was complimented for his acting; only then could we see daylight between the star and the role.)

If we are to consider the meaning of a film we need to dispense with literary-based notions of character as a receptacle into which the star disappears. We need to take account of the meaning of the film's stars and the way those meanings contribute to characterization. The star can change meaning over time; for instance, the casting of Jane Fonda in the mid 1960s and her casting now will carry different meanings. Fonda began her career as a sex symbol

13 In magazines stars' images circulate even more vigorously outside the cinemas

and only gradually modified the kind of characters she played. By altering the nature of the characterizations or representations to which she lent herself, she altered her own meaning to the point where she could play the tortured Bree Daniels in *Klute*, and the more interpretative roles of the last ten years. Fonda's early films, such as *Barbarella* or *La Ronde*, make a different kind of sense now that she has changed the nature of *her* meanings (Dyer 1982).

Dyer reveals just how much work the audience (as well as the film-maker) accomplish in constructing character in films. So much of what constitutes a major character is *already* there to be appropriated to the film's meaning by the audience, and by the film-maker in the act of casting. Casting can be the most important act in the film-maker's construction of a character, since a well-judged piece of casting can mobilize all the meanings carried by a particular star and inject them into the representation of the character on the screen. If we cast Richard Gere, we do not have to convince the audience that the character is attractive to women; if we cast Woody Allen, we might have to demonstrate that. (Alternatively, we might have a lot of work to do in any script that asked Richard Gere to play a neurotic, garrulous, New York intellectual.) The problem of sexual desire for Dustin Hoffman's character in *Tootsie* is established by the casting of Jessica Lange, as well as by the means of her representation – glamorized lighting and soft focus, for instance. As we track the audience's relationship to a film through the star, we not only track a set of identifications with a star, but a set of meanings already encoded into that star's representation on the screen. Assumptions about the nature of film characterization – as one-dimensional or 'flat' for instance – need to be interrogated by way of an admission that the face of the star is part of film characterization, too. Often the power of the star to carry contributory meanings relieves the script of the burden of constructing a complex character. The complexity can be achieved visually through the casting of the appropriate performer.

A further aspect of Dyer's work deals with the wider social meanings of stars. Stars are constructed in contradictory ways that emphasize their typicality *and* their individuality. For the star to attract an audience there must be some representativeness, some apparently recognizable element which an audience can use to link the star with themselves. Bryan Brown (*Winter of our Dreams*, *Breaker Morant*, *FX*, *Parker*) is seen in his home country as a positive representation of the absolutely typical Australian male.

Yet for him to be a star (both at home and internationally) he has to transcend this Australian-ness and generate a richness and individuality. Star status can itself invest the ordinary with mythic status – James Stewart made a career out of depicting the ordinary individual who, blessed only with determination, had the power to affect society. Star status carries with it the potential to individualize and particularize even the most general of social types. Dyer talks of stars 'transcending' their type by being, paradoxically, both representative and unique – lifelike and larger than life. Clearly there are limits to this effect if a film is to be understood, but it does mean that a character which is 'flat' in the script can be 'round' as portrayed by the particularly signifying actor.

The final point to be made about the ways in which an audience will understand the role of the star refers to the social and ideological meanings that he or she carries. Since stars are iconic representations of recognizable social types, they are composed within the field of dominant and competing definitions of society. Dyer says that one of the types that the star embodies is that of 'the type of the individual himself': they 'embody that particular conception of what it is to be human that characterises our culture' (1982: 111). The depth of affection certain stars excite in their audiences is related to their personal signification, for instance as a national type. Judy Garland and Mickey Rooney's Andy Hardy films signified one version of America, David Niven (in, for example, *Casino Royale*) a version of Britain, Chips Rafferty (in, for example, *The Rats of Tobruk*) a version of Australia. This function of the star is ultimately ideological and is implicated in the relationship between film and the idea of the nation which is taken up in Chapter 6.

Before leaving this topic, it is worth demonstrating the kind of information such an approach produces. Dyer's second book, *Heavenly Bodies* (1986), examines three major Hollywood stars in order to show what they meant to their audiences. His treatment of Paul Robeson, Marilyn Monroe, and Judy Garland reveals both the ways in which the star enacts or mobilizes dominant ideas (of, for instance, sexuality in Monroe's case), and also the ways in which a star can be taken up by sections of the community and given specialized meanings: the gay community's adoption of Judy Garland shows how subcultures can 'make over' even the most mainstream of images to their own use.

In his analysis of Marilyn Monroe, Dyer tries to explain how she came to be *the* sex-symbol, probably for all time. Firstly, he makes connections between broader social movements during the 1950s, when Monroe was at the peak of her popularity, and the particular meanings she carried as a star. Sexuality itself, he argues, was an issue at the time:

> sex was seen as perhaps the most important thing in life in fifties America. Certain publishing events suggest this: the two Kinsey reports (on men, 1948; on women, 1953), the first issues of *Confidential* in 1951 and *Playboy* in 1953, both to gain very rapidly in circulation; best-selling novels such as *From Here to Eternity* (1951), *A House is Not a Home* (1953) . . . *Peyton Place* (1956) . . . not to mention the thrillers of Mickey Spillane. Betty Friedan, in *The Feminine Mystique*, quotes a survey of Albert Ellis, published in *The Folklore of Sex* in 1961, which shows that 'in American media there were more than 2.5 times as many references to sex in 1960 as in 1950'.
>
> (Dyer 1986: 24–5)

Dyer does not see Monroe's popularity, or her specific meaning as a sex symbol, as a simple reflection of such trends, however. In fact, he moves away from this kind of broad social analysis and turns to an examination of the 1950s 'discourses' of sexuality, discourses which are employed in the construction of her meaning as a star. Dyer defines this use of the term 'discourse' as referring to those 'clusters of ideas, notions, feelings, images, attitudes and assumptions that, taken together, make up distinctive ways of thinking and feeling about things, of making a particular sense of the world' (p. 19). He connects the ways the 1950s had of making 'a particular sense' of sex with the signification of Marilyn Monroe on the screen and in her wider public image as a star.

In Dyer's account, 1950s America had discovered sexuality as *the* key to the self, and as the central aspect of adult life. Certainly, sexuality assumes a new cultural prominence. For example, with the decline of the family film and the rise of the adult film in response to television's capture of the family audience, mainstream cinema became more 'daring' and 'explicit' in its treatment of sex. The arrival of *Playboy* is a convenient marker of this new interest in sexuality, and Monroe is herself closely connected with the new magazine as she featured in its first nude centrefold. This created something of a scandal, even though the photo used was from a calendar that Monroe had posed for well before she became a star. Monroe is more than an illustration to *Playboy*,

14   The ultimate star image: Marilyn Monroe (courtesy of the National Film and Sound Archive of Australia)

however; according to Dyer, Monroe's image enacted 'as no one else was doing at the time, the particular definitions of sexuality which *Playboy* was proselytising' (p. 28). These definitions were produced through discourses which represent sexuality as natural, guilt-free, non-exploitative, and as somehow connected with psychological health.

Dyer goes into this at some length (pp. 27–42), but a summary of part of his argument will be sufficient to demonstrate its value. He refers to the scandal over the nude centrefold as a point where Monroe's meaning is clearly available for inspection. When Monroe was challenged by the media about the nude picture (unheard-of for a major star at the time), she refused to accept any guilt. 'I've done nothing wrong', she said, and when asked by reporters what she had on when the photo was taken replied, 'I had the radio on'. As Dyer says, this is a 'classic dumb-blonde one-liner' which 'implies a refusal or inability to answer the question at the level of prurience at which it was asked'. As Dyer continues to argue, this guiltlessness, naturalness, and the absence of prurience in her attitude to sex, is tied in precisely with the *Playboy* philosophy. *Playboy* represented its sexual discourses as progressive, attacking rigid, bourgeois, and hypocritical sexual values, and recognizing the 'naturalness' of the sex drive. Sexuality was thus disconnected from the sinful, temptress image of, say, the heroines of *films noirs*, such as Barbara Stanwyck or Joan Crawford, and in its place came a sexually desirable but unthreatening 'natural' sensualist: Marilyn Monroe. Even the apparent dumbness of the 'dumb blonde' was a sign of the natural; if she was 'untouched by the rationality of the world', she was also untouched by its corruption. In Monroe a linkage is established between sexuality and innocence, and this linkage – perhaps more than any other – explains her dramatic power as a popular image.

Dyer does not stop here (although we will). He investigates the meaning of blondeness, of the conventional open-mouthed poses for photo sessions, and of the way in which Monroe was incorporated into popular conceptions of psychology and psychoanalysis of the time. The ambiguity of her image for feminists – an image used to subject women and a person who was herself exploited – is also dealt with. The real value of Dyer's analysis, though, is that it demonstrates how much of the meaning of a film is brought into the cinema with its audience and, conversely, the cultural power of the meanings generated by the movies.

THE FILM EXPERIENCE

Discussion of the relationship between the audience and what it sees on the screen inevitably leads us to re-examine just what it is that constitutes the experience of going to the cinema. In order to differentiate film from television, theorists as well as the industry have talked of film-going as an 'event'. The act of going out is itself intrinsic to the event of cinema-going; also significant is cinema's role as what Jowett and Linton (1980) call a 'social integrator', a way of signalling that the individual is not too deviant in cultural activities. The pleasures of the evening are not exhausted by the experience of watching the film, and cinema-going is most often a group activity – rarely do people go to the cinema by themselves. A sense of release and separation from the world is provided even by films which we do not much like. The charge of escapism which is often levelled at film is probably based on the sense of separation from reality, which is highlighted as we leave the cinema, as much as on a close analysis of the content of the majority of films.

The specific characteristics of the film experience have provoked a great deal of analysis. We sit in the dark, within a group but still separated from them by the fact that they are not easily visible; we watch realistic images which are nevertheless vastly oversized representations of the real; we sit in comfortable seats, our attention focused on the screen and with no competitors for that attention. The avidity of our gaze is inevitable; the physical structure of the theatre itself implies the strength of the audience's desire to consume the sounds and images which will be projected in front of them. Sociologists such as Andrew Tudor (1974) have argued that the intensity of the image/sound message, the comfort of the viewer, and the heightened sense of occasion, all make the viewer more susceptible to the power of the message. High-culture critics of popular culture have employed this avenue of attack to raise worries about the psychological effects (or, more accurately, the ideological effects) of the medium.

There is certainly an intense vicarious involvement offered to the cinema-goer. Further, the fact that the medium is one of representation rather than an unmediated perception of the real is deliberately buried and effaced by the mechanisms of the medium. Early Cinerama sold itself by its ability to appear to replicate as closely as possible our experience of the real world and then amplify it – to make it *more than real*. The Cinerama rendition of the roller-coaster ride replicated our perceptions of the actual experience so precisely that viewers would feel sick; it created the sensation of speed in the audience as palpably as if they were on the roller-coaster rather than in the theatre. At such moments, the apparatus of the cinema disappears; any thought of mediation is banished by the fact that one's body is telling one that this is *really* happening. The Cinerama image is only an image, but we react to it as if it were more than that.

This blurring of the boundaries between the imaginary and the real is at the heart of the cinema experience. Representation appears as perception. Metz (1982) has called the filmed image 'the imaginary signifier', referring to the fact that the reality which the filmed images call up is always absent, 'present' only in our imaginations. This fact has led researchers to examine the similarities between viewing a film and an analogous condition, dreaming. The analogy is very close in some aspects. Dreams don't 'really' happen although we might experience them as if they did; contradictorily, even though the *content* of the dream may not have happened, the *dream experience itself* did. Like films, dreams have the capacity to express thought through images; they also have a tendency towards narrative (even generic) structures, and give the effect of seeming more than real. Jean-Louis Baudry (1974) sees film producing, through the darkness of the theatre, the spectator's relative passivity, and, through the hypnotic effect of flickering light and shadows, what he calls an artificially regressive state. This condition mimics that of dreaming. According to Baudry, cinema, like dreaming, is regressive in that it calls up the unconscious processes of the mind and favours what Freud calls the pleasure principle over the reality principle. Without going into Freudian theories of the structure of the personality, this implies a slip back into the childish, immature version of the self where our wants and desires (the forces behind the pleasure principle) dominate our personalities at the expense of contextual, ethical, and social considerations (the reality principle). In such a formulation, film is dangerous, and this view has been used to support anxiety about whether it is healthy to expose children to the medium.

There is a large literature on these aspects of audience involvement with the image. Metz argues that film narrative itself possesses some of the characteristics of dreams, and that it is dealt with by its audiences in similar, if unconscious, ways. The dream analogy can be a useful one, although it is limited – for one thing – by the fact that films are not only images; they are also sound. Further, the process of decoding film languages is as much conscious and social as it is unconscious and presocial. However, there are issues raised by Metz, in particular, which have been followed up.

Metz (1982: 92) says that when he is in the cinema as a member of the audience, he 'watches' and he 'helps'. The cinema audience watches because the image is itself seductive, larger than life, an object of desire. The audience thus concentrates on looking. But the structure of film narrative is such that its meaning has to be actively constructed by the viewers as they watch. The term 'suture' (Dayan 1974), for instance, explains how each shot in a film is continually involved in constructing the relationships which will help the film make sense – relationships between one shot and the next, one sequence and its adjacent sequences, and so on. Because the meaning of one shot is deferred until we see how it is 'fixed' (or stitched together – 'sutured') by its relation to the following shot, cinema is able to hide its method of constructing itself. This deferral of meaning, the closing of gaps by the viewers, means that they drive the narrative forward in order to understand what they have seen. Viewers are diverted from examining the means of construction by concentrating on the meaning.

Film viewers do not know all they need to know until the film ends. This exacerbates the pressure towards completion, towards mastery of the narrative – 'helping'. This mastery is of course always promised and usually delivered since the viewer is usually the point at which the film makes sense. But there is a deep contradiction that again reminds one of dreaming, in that spectators are drawn between, on the one hand, their desire for the image, their luxuriating in this amplification of the real and its celebration of the power of their gaze; and, on the other hand, their desire for domination of the narrative, for their achievement of mastery. The result is that we both want the film to end – to gain knowledge of it – and wish that it would continue to offer its objects of desire. Ellis (1982: 81) puts it this way:

> Entertainment cinema offers the possibility of seeing events and comprehending them from a position of separation and mastery. The film is offered to the spectator, but the spectator does not have anything to offer the film apart from the desire to see and hear. Hence the spectator's position is one of power, specifically the power to understand events rather than to change them. This is the position of mastery that can shade into

fascination, into the fetishistic desire to abolish the very distance and separation that makes the process of seeing possible.

As he says, the audience desires to 'enter' the film, to disrupt even the minimal boundaries which divide the imaginary and the real in the cinema. This occurs at an unconscious level, and underlines just how essential it is to have some understanding of the unconscious process of watching a film. We need to introduce some of the uses made of psychoanalysis to explain this process.

THE FILM SPECTATOR AND PSYCHOANALYSIS

Film theory has become greatly interested in psychoanalysis. Of course, psychoanalysis is highly interested in dreams, and the analogies between film and dreams make Freudian theories of the operation of the unconscious an inevitable avenue for researchers to explore. The nature of film's fascination – its collapsing of the boundaries of the real – is a further invitation to psychoanalysis. If Freud held that the gap between the real and the imaginary (what we see and what we might imagine for ourselves) was the location of desire, then film does occupy that gap. What most of the responses to these issues have produced is a series of theories about the processes through which the audience identify with what they see on the screen. These processes are seen to be analogous to the ways in which the audience members construct their own identities within society.

Psychoanalytic theory has emphasized the importance of the 'look', the gaze of the audience. This is reflected in its references to the audience as 'the spectator'. The power of the individual's look is important within Freudian and post-Freudian theory since it is part of the individual's self-definition and relationship to his or her environment. So audiences 'look', and they also 'spectate'. Audiences are 'separated' from the film because it represents actions which are going on for their benefit, but as if they were not there. However, as agents for understanding the film, and as observers who can see but not be seen, they are in a position of considerable power. Freudian theory describes such a position as that of the voyeur, who 'makes an object of' those caught unwittingly in the power of his gaze. The voyeuristic look is one of the pleasures an audience finds in the cinema.

This may not be entirely accurate, as we shall see, because our voyeur knows that while the actors may not be present they *do* know that they are to be watched. So they exhibit themselves to the spectator rather than unwittingly reveal themselves. A passage from Christian Metz outlines just how complicated this relationship is:

> The cinema was born much later than the theatre, in a period when social life was deeply marked by the notion of the *individual* (or its more elevated version, 'personality'), when there were no longer any slaves to enable 'free men' to form a relatively homogeneous group. . . . The cinema is made for the private individual and in the spectator's voyeurism there is no need for him to be seen (if it is dark in the cinema, the visible is entirely confined to the screen). . . . It is enough . . . that the actor should behave as though he were not to be seen (and therefore as though he did not see his voyeur), that he should go about his ordinary business and pursue his existence as foreseen by the fiction of the film, that he should carry on his antics in a closed room, taking the utmost care not to notice that a glass rectangle has been set into one of the walls, and that he lives in a kind of aquarium, one which is simply a little less generous with its 'apertures' than real aquariums.
>
> (1982: 96)

Psychoanalytic theory has taken us some way into this aquarium, and I review some of its achievements and concerns in the following section. The most central of these revolve around the problem we have already introduced – the nature of the audience's identification with the image.

AUDIENCE IDENTIFICATION

We have always been told that we 'identify with' or see ourselves in characters on the screen. Screen heroes and heroines are widely held to offer some kind of wish fulfilment, and our admiration for one or other of them is assumed to be the expression of a wish we might, even unconsciously, want fulfilled. However, we also know that we do not only enjoy movies which invite this kind of identification; in fact, the film experience in either case is not markedly different. Psychoanalysis has revealed two main categories of audience identification; and neither of them has much to do with conventional identification with the hero or heroine.

Firstly, Metz (1982) and others have argued that the nature of cinema-going is such that the very apparatus of the cinema invites us to identify with it. I have already referred to the way in which the development of the camera was encouraged by an ideology of individualism, and explained how its invention incorporates the view that the individual's perception is the organizing principle of reality. When the camera is received as the viewing perspective on a series of projected images, it becomes a proxy for our eyes. Although there are such things as 'point-of-view' shots, where the camera is clearly presenting a series of images from the point of view of a specific character within the film, in most cases it takes the point of view of the narrating authority – the organizing principle of the film – which we identify as that of the audience (us). Metz argues that if we wish to make sense of the film, to achieve mastery over it, it is this point of view with which we must identify ourselves. The camera (and by extension, the projector) becomes our eyes, and when we wish not to see what it shows us – gore in a horror movie, for instance – we shut our eyes and turn our heads. Our processes of perception are dramatized, made material, in the beam of light from the projector streaming down from behind our heads in the darkened theatre. As we see the film as our perception, rather than someone else's representation, we collapse the distinction between our eyes and the projection apparatus. This may not ring entirely true, since many films and even some genres depend on a degree of separation between the audience and the image. Further, the argument entirely discounts the role of sound. Nevertheless, Metz argues persuasively that we 'identify' with the mechanisms of the cinema because they become, as it were, extensions of ourselves.

The second category of spectator identification with narrative film is more difficult to simplify. This is the spectator's identification with more or less everything that he or she sees on the screen. Not only do we identify with our heroes and heroines, but with all the characters at various points in the narrative. This is a consequence of seeing the screen as if it were, in some respects, a mirror of ourselves and of our world.

The post-Freudian theorist Jacques Lacan developed a most influential description of an aspect of childhood development which he called the 'mirror stage'. This is the point when a young child first recognizes itself in the mirror and realizes it has an identity separate from that of the mother. In recognizing an image of itself, and in forming a fascination for that image, the child begins to construct an identity. However, what children see, what they can only *ever* see, is an image of themselves – a representation. Here begins the process of human misunderstanding and self-delusion: our egoistic identification with the image of ourselves is always in some sense illusory.

Nevertheless, the image of oneself is fascinating, irresistible to the child and to the narcissistic aspects of adult personalities. As Dudley Andrew (1984: 149) has put it:

> Our fascination with films is now thought to be not a fascination with particular characters and intrigues so much as a fascination with the image itself, based on a primal 'mirror stage' in our psychic growth. Just as we were, when infants, confronted with the gloriously complete view of ourselves in the mirror, so now we identify with the gloriously complete presentation of a spectacle on the screen.

Despite its highly technologized character, the pleasure film offers is, then, almost primal. There seem to be aspects of the process of identifying with film which emanate from our most basic drives. The various categories into which Freud divides the 'look' in his discussion of the components of human sexuality have their parallel in the pleasures that we obtain from film. There is the narcissistic (seeing oneself reflected on the screen), the voyeuristic (enjoying the power of another's image on the screen), and the fetishistic (a way of exaggerating the power of material things or people in order to deal with one's fear of them). All are expressions of human sexuality, or displacements of desire; all can be argued to offer the means of identification between the film and the audience.

This idea of the mirror stage might seem a little far-fetched, but there are many strong arguments for relating the pleasure derived from film to that primitive pleasure felt in the mirror stage. Of course, the analogy does have its limits; it could be argued that in the cinema one sees everything *but* oneself. Perhaps the real benefit of this analogy is its highlighting of the confusion between perception and reality that is common to the construction of the self and to our understanding of the narrative film. In this commonality we can see an ancient psychic root beneath this most modern of narrative systems.

Psychoanalysis also reveals other pre-cinematic patterns which determine the audience–image relationship. Definitions of human sexuality are clearly of interest here, since this is an area where the notion of voyeurism, for one, requires little demonstration. The deployment of the female form and the adoption of the point of view of the unseen male spectator have marked much Hollywood film; they are central to films as otherwise different as *The Seven Year Itch* and *10*, and are explicitly interrogated in Brian De Palma's films, *Dressed to Kill* and *Body Double*. Feminist work on the representation of the female in film has focused, predictably enough, on the commodification of the female body; the exploitation of the female body as a cinema spectacle; and the denial that contemporary cinema has made any significant change to these patterns of representation and exploitation.

Laura Mulvey's (1975) work has been particularly influential. She, like Metz, argues that the fascination of film is 'reinforced by pre-existing patterns of fascination already at work within the individual subject and the social formations that moulded him' (p. 305). She appropriates Freud's definition of the look, and claims that cinema is essentially involved with gratifying the desire to look – 'scopophilia'. But this is not a simple matter. As we have said, cinema constructs the audience as voyeur – offering the pleasure of using another as an object of stimulation through sight – and it also constructs the audience as narcissistic – identifying with the object seen. The first construction explains, for instance, the development of the spectacle of the female body in films for the voyeuristic male audience. The second, however, would appear to contradict the first. Presumably, the male does not identify narcissistically with the female object of his voyeuristic look. Similarly, a female spectator is unlikely to identify with the object of the voyeuristic look. Mulvey argues that the narrative film solves this contradiction by representing the female as the object of desire on the one hand, and as the passive object of the film's action on the other. The audience identify with the male hero's desire for the female, voyeuristically, and with his active resolution of the narrative, narcissistically. Consequently, women are rarely essential to film plots (as they are essential to film spectacle), or represented as able to resolve narrative dilemmas unaided. There is no place for the female character actively to drive the movie's narrative and thus compete for the audience's narcissistic identification. The male view, Mulvey argues, is the only point from which the pleasure of film narrative can be derived, and so the pleasure of female film audiences is phallocentric.

This is only part of Mulvey's extensive critique of Hollywood narratives, but it has been extremely important. It is widely accepted now that most mainstream cinema, and particularly Hollywood cinema, is constructed for 'the male gaze': that is, the dominant viewpoint to which the narratives address themselves is masculine, and film's visual pleasures (including the spectacle of the female body) are primarily for men as well. Much of the work Mulvey's original essay inspired has examined the function of the male gaze in specific groups or genres of films. Linda Williams (1984) shows how many films do indeed recognize women's power and depict them as making use of it, only to then punish them for doing so. A staple of suspense thrillers and horror films (two examples Williams cites are *Psycho* and *Dressed to Kill*) is the moment 'when the woman looks' – when, despite what she knows is likely to be waiting for her, and despite her 'female vulnerability', she dares to look behind 'that' door. At such moments women might be regarded as attempting to appropriate the male gaze, Williams argues. The consequence is some kind of narrative penalty – often they are made the object of the film's violence or terror unless or until they are rescued by a male. One could think of many further examples of this: from the many Hitchcock thrillers where the woman attempts to free herself from the control of a man by 'looking' for herself (*Suspicion*, *Notorious*, *Spellbound* or *Rebecca*, for instance to such recent examples as *Fatal Attraction*). In her book, *The Desire to Desire* (1988), Mary Ann Doane examines what one would expect to be a less masculinist genre, the 'women's films' from the 1940s. Doane discovers that here, too, female characters are continually the object of the controlling gaze of the male characters – as the patients of understanding male doctors, for example, or as endangered females in gothic melodrama. Doane maintains that in such films desire itself is effectively masculine. The women are denied desires of their own, left only with the desire to be the object of masculine desire (the 'desire to be desired') or, at best, yearning to be allowed the 'desire to desire'.

While such work has become a central element within accounts of popular cinema today, there is debate within feminist film theory about how comprehensive and uncontested the male gaze actually is. As we saw in Chapter 4, the strong central characters in

15   Sigourney Weaver as Ripley in *Aliens* (© 1986 Twentieth Century
Fox Film Corporation. All rights reserved)

the *Alien* series and *Terminator 2* are among the cases where a female does take charge of the narrative without becoming masculinized and without being punished for it. Tania Modleski (1988) has taken issue with Mulvey's readings of Hitchcock's films as voyeuristic and sadistic in their treatment of women, by finding in many of his films some limited expression of female desire. Following Teresa de Lauretis (1984) and Mulvey's own more recent work (1989), Modleski argues that Hitchcock's films are much more ambivalent than has been suggested: that 'despite the often considerable violence with which women are treated in Hitchcock's films, they remain resistant to patriarchal assimilation' (1988: 3). Gaylyn Studlar (1985) has further contested Mulvey's assumption that the only pleasures with which a film spectator might identify are the (masculine and sadistic) pleasures of control, as against the (feminine and masochistic) pleasures of submission. A common element in arguments such as Modleski's and Studlar's is their resistance to an undifferentiated notion of the sense individual female members of the audience might make of the films they see. Simply, they are wary of arguments which assume all women will read these texts the same way.

A consequence of such critiques is the suggestion that mainstream cinema might also address, albeit in a subordinated manner, a 'female gaze'. This has occasioned a move away from psychoanalytic explanations towards a focus on the socially constructed, active female reader of texts – the 'female spectator'. Typically, such work foregrounds the social, cultural or historical factors in our understanding of films in order to account for the pleasures female spectators derive from popular cinema. Deidre Pribram (1988: 5) talks of the importance of emphasizing women's 'presence in, rather than absence from, the "cinematic experience"', and the essays in her collection emphasize the multiplicity of relationships women negotiate with film and television texts. Miriam Hansen (1989: 169) investigates the difference between the 'textually constructed spectator' (the female viewer Mulvey reads from the film text, for instance) and the 'actual' moviegoer, in order to also counterpose the 'social, collective, experiential dimension of cinematic reception' against exclusively psychoanalytic accounts. Her provocation for this comes from watching some old Valentino films which, she argues, while obviously aligning the male gaze with narrative and sexual power, also blatantly displayed the body of the star to the desiring gaze of millions of female fans. Hansen's work probably represents the extreme perimeter of this line of enquiry as the implications emerging from it lead us out of the domain of psychoanalytic theory and into that of film historiography.

DESIRE AND THE IMAGE

There have been many criticisms of the theoretical positions summarized in the preceding section. The aural aspects of film, as we have seen, disturb the dream analogy, and also shatter the comprehensiveness of Lacan's mirror analogy. Any sense of the differences between films tends to disappear before psychoanalytic theory. The dream analogy also tends to make film simply the bearer of fantasies; just as critics in other art forms have found this position hard to accept, film theorists have produced arguments countering it. The use of the analogy of the dream or the mirror as an explanatory device, as if it were a method of analysis, has been exposed to criticism. It is at the very least reductive to approach the film audience solely through the filter of the unconscious since a single system of signification is thus set aside from the many others which also contribute to the audience's experience of film.

Where psychoanalysis has been most suggestive is in its attempt to describe the audience's desire for the film text. Dudley Andrew, himself a stern critic of psychoanalytic theory, presents a thoroughly psychoanalytic description of the desire for the image:

> Desiring to possess the film, we are confined to merely viewing it. Consequently, the successful film can never ultimately satisfy us; rather, it rewards our passion to see by offering us still more to see until we are thrown beyond the bounds of its narrative space and out into the queue waiting for the next film to light up on the screen, to light up the cavern of our psyches.
>
> (1984: 148)

As his closing clauses emphasize, the action which draws us into the cinema is on the screen as well as in our psyches. He emphasizes later (p. 152) that the 'psychic dimension of cinematic meaning is paramount but only as regulated and shaped in cinematic discourse'. The importance of the particular text is not to be overlooked. The specificities of the text add up to what Metz (1982: 92) calls a formula 'for granting a wish that was never formulated in the first place', an admission of the power of the text to call the audience into *its* unconscious, as it were.

It is worth remembering, as we move from this topic, that film theory's attempt to deploy versions of the Freudian understanding of pleasure is by no means universally accepted or universally useful. And there are other ways of thinking about pleasure. Roland Barthes (1975), for instance, located pleasure in the body in a much more physical way than Freud, seeing it as the individual's last defence against the persuasion of language and the consensual bullying of ideologies. For Barthes, pleasure is a potentially political force which can be resistant to control. However, neither Freud's nor Barthes's approach seems to have a comprehensive explanatory power. In film, the visceral effects of the car chase, the roller-coaster ride, the coming together of vision and music in a romantic conclusion (say, at the end of *An Officer and a Gentleman*), occur at moments when the body takes over and dominates our sensation of responding to the film. We experience that takeover as pleasurable. Barthesian notions of pleasure seem inappropriate here; his view of pleasure foregrounds the unconventional, the unpredictable, the ambiguous, and such moments are (at least) a complex mixture of these attributes *and* their opposites.

There are different experiences that we might describe as pleasurable, even in the movies. One frequently forgotten aspect is the pleasure we find in the familiar, in seeing a convention faithfully played out so that Richard Gere *does* carry Debra Winger out of the factory to a new life (unimagined, fortunately) in *An Officer and a Gentleman*; there is the pleasure in confirming, through one's mastery of the film, one's membership in the culture; there is the pleasure in watching fashions and images for their own sake, or as a kind of shopping trip in order to compose one's own representation of oneself; there is a pleasure in the text which comes not only from recognizing the new and surprising but from recognizing intertextual links and generic conventions as well as their disruption; there is a further pleasure in watching a film or series of films as parts of the continuing development of the star as a sign (*Lethal Weapon*, for Mel Gibson watchers, offers such a pleasure).

These are among the characteristic pleasures of popular culture and they are all (potentially) implicated in the audience's decision to see a film and in what they do with the film when they see it.

They are social, cultural pleasures, appropriated by individuals for their own use but in no sense originating with each individual. They are pleasures offered by other social practices within popular culture too, and therefore reveal how the social practice of film is enclosed within *other* practices, within other systems of meaning.

AUDIENCES, TEXTS, AND MEANINGS

It is clear that we need to be aware of both textual and 'extra-textual' factors in any audience's understanding of a film. The film's meaning is not simply a property of its particular arrangement of elements; its meaning is produced in relation to an audience, not independently. Once we realize this we find it possible to accept that audiences may find a multiplicity of meanings in any one film text; its meaning is not necessarily 'fixed', unchangeable.

One of the results of the break between film studies and a pre-eminently aesthetic tradition of film appreciation is the abandonment of the idea that there was a core of meaning in a film which the audience had to uncover. Within film studies, and cultural studies generally, it is now more customary to talk of 'meanings' than of Meaning. Meanings are seen as the products of an audience's reading rather than as an essential property of the film text itself. Audiences make films mean; they don't merely recognize the meanings already secreted in them.

This does cause problems at the practical level. Most of us watching a film will feel that there is some limit to the kind of readings to which it might be subjected. Certain sets of conventions, such as those of genre, seem to exist precisely to organize, determine, or otherwise channel the audience's potentially various responses into a homogeneous, single point of view. There is a degree of dislocation between the theory and the practice of watching a film. On the one hand, the audience's readings of a film occupy a theoretical field of almost infinite possibility; on the other hand, in practice we find that while the audience's readings may differ, they will still be contained within a relatively discrete range of possibilities. Cultural studies' attempts to deal with this have employed a range of tactics, from recovering the idea that the text is in control of its readers, to the dethroning of the text in order to see it as entirely the product of socially formed reading practices.

Stuart Hall's earlier work (1977) on television and the press is important here. He argued that the formal properties of media texts were organized in order to 'prefer' one way of being read. This 'preferred' reading was also the one which was most in accord with the meanings produced by the dominant ideological systems. This did not preclude there being other ways of reading a text, however. Although audiences might recognize the preferred reading as one that was implicit in the text's formal properties, they could still refuse that reading for an alternative. This could be 'negotiated' (accepting some, but not all, of the principles behind the preferred reading); or it could be an 'oppositional' reading which wholly rejected the preferred reading position. Whatever reading position was adopted, however, it always articulated itself through a relationship to the dominant ideological system. A crude example of this process would be the way audiences might react to a party political broadcast. For one audience member, the speaker might represent the favoured political party and so engender little argument; for another, the speaker might only intersect with his or her value systems at certain points; and for a third, the speaker might typify all that must be resisted and opposed.

I still find the preferred reading a useful concept. But it does present problems. Firstly, the idea of a preferred reading is not totally separable from that of a 'true' meaning. The text is still seen as the ultimate dictator of its readings. What is offered is an account of 'different readings of the same text'. It is important to recognize that if we believe that meaning is to some extent indeterminate, then 'different readings' of a film will actually produce 'different' films. Secondly, the functioning of ideology through texts and readers is now seen to be a more complex and less determined process than Hall originally suggested. Hall (1982) has himself contributed to changes in the way in which the work of ideology has been defined.

Perhaps the clearest countermove to Hall emerges from the growing tradition of ethnographic research into television. This tradition is usually exemplified by Dave Morley's work (1980) on the British magazine programme *Nationwide*. Morley reverses the relations suggested in the Hall model by seeing social formations such as class, gender, subculture, ethnicity, and occupation as the key determinants of the audience's opinions about *Nationwide*. Extra-textual factors are thus seen to be driving the reading of texts, and there is the sound of a radical explosion of possible readings as we discover more social categories into which we might divide our audiences. While Morley certainly demolished assumptions of a mass, homogeneous audience soaking up TV indiscriminately, he still offered an account of different versions of the 'same text', in conjunction with a reductive view of what constitutes the differences between audience members.

Neither of these approaches is entirely satisfactory, although both remind us that audiences read films through their specific forms *and* through cultural determinants. The difficulty remaining is to get the balance between audience and film, history and text, 'just right', so that we can see texts and readers as 'mutual supports of each other'.

This last phrase is drawn from Bennett and Woollacott's *Bond and Beyond: the Political Career of a Popular Hero* (1987), and it is to their work that I now wish to turn. *Bond and Beyond* is so far the most complete cultural studies account of an aspect of film and popular culture. In it, the authors examine the James Bond phenomenon: the books, the films, the stars, the character, the audiences, the production practices, and, most of all, the meanings it has generated. As they admit, Bond is a little *passé* now; the film audiences are growing ever younger, and the backlog of novels is almost gone. But it is an important location for the examination of the ways in which a fictional character can become a popular hero through the specific interactions between books and films, magazine interviews and stars, texts and history. Although film study is not its primary aim, *Bond and Beyond* offers benefits for the discipline because it deals with the relationships between popular texts and their audiences.

The first move Bennett and Woollacott make is to extend the meaning of a term we have already met: intertextuality. As they rightly point out, this term conventionally refers to the relationships between one text and another. They introduce a third term, inter-textuality, to denote the complex of relationships between texts and the social conditions of their production and consumption. They challenge the idea that the meaning of a film might be fixed, by proving that the meaning of James Bond as a popular hero has never been fixed. The book is largely devoted to chronicling and analysing the changes in the meaning of James Bond.

Because they examine a whole range of texts – a mini-genre of Bond films, novels, and articles – Bennett and Woollacott see Bond as the product of *all* of the 'texts of Bond' rather than any single one. A change in the way Bond is constructed in one text affects the potential of all the rest. For instance, the image of Bond apparently conjured up in 'the mind's eye' by the novels is quite different to that represented by Sean Connery in the first film. Yet now, the authors argue, the mind's eye image incorporates Connery, even when the novels are being read.

Bond and Beyond presents a clear account of the way that Bond's meanings have shifted; how meanings have been bred, rather than contained, by these texts over Bond's thirty-year career as a popular hero. Before the films were produced, Bond was an entirely literary figure. He was specifically British, tied into a mythology of nationhood which constructed Britain as the cutting edge of the western world, and which denied the decline of its empire and influence on world politics. Bond was also politically chauvinistic and sexually exploitative; attacks were made on the gratuitous sex and violence of the novels well before the films were produced.

The first Bond film, *Dr No*, was released in 1962, and this began what Bennett and Woollacott call the 'ideological remodelling' of the hero. First, Bond was extracted from the cold war climate of the novels from the 1950s, and given a context more appropriate to 1960s *détente*. From 1961, Fleming's novels abandoned the hitherto central ideological opposition between the Soviet Union and the west, and pitted Bond against the international criminal organization, SPECTRE. The subsequent partial 'depoliticization' was aimed at broadening the hero's appeal for movie-goers, and giving the films (as the producer put it) 'legs worldwide'. Secondly, Bond's affiliation with a past, Establishment Britain was attenuated so that he could become the icon of the 'swinging Britain' of the mid-1960s:

> Bond provided a mythic encapsulation of the then prominent ideological themes of classlessness and modernity, a key cultural marker of the claim that Britain had escaped the blinkered, class-bound perspectives of its traditional ruling elites and was in the process of being thoroughly modernised as a result of the implementation of a new meritocratic style of cultural and political leadership, middle class and professional rather than aristocratic and amateur.
>
> (Bennett and Woollacott 1987: 34–5)

Similarly, 'the Bond girls' who partnered the hero were used to represent a new, modern version of female sexuality – 'liberated from the constraints of family, marriage and domesticity'. In many ways, Bond was quite central to popular culture of the time. As the authors put it, he was a 'sign of the times', but a sign that was to shift from one meaning to another.

James Bond was less central to the popular culture of the 1970s. Bennett and Woollacott argue that there is a ritualistic aspect to the figure at that time which was connected to the key element in the films, the demonstration of high technology in action. The equipping of the Aston Martin, for instance, became a conventional ritual in the films while ideological interest in Bond himself became more muted and even secondary. Relations between Bond and his girls were also realigned during this period so that the liberated woman of the 1960s found herself forced to accept domination of one kind or another. There is a regressive impetus behind the structure of gender relations in the Bond films of the 1970s and, as we move into the 1980s, a deal of confusion as to just what the audience expected of Bond and his women. In the 1980s, the authors say, 'Bond no longer occupied centre-stage within the re-organized system of inter-textual relations which characterised the popular culture of the period' (p. 39). Bond films are still an institution, but have less cultural power than before. The hero himself has less power within the narrative, too. *A View to a Kill* has Grace Jones's May Day dominating Bond (sexually and professionally) to an unprecedented degree. As a result, *Bond and Beyond* points out, she dies. But the shifts in the way the films represent Bond offer hints of a widening gap between Bond, his producers, and his audience over the last few years.

This brief summary outlines a history of a set of texts, and a history of the meanings which have been given to these texts. Bennett and Woollacott use such histories to make the point that both films and their audiences are, as it were, culturally operated; what a film means can and does change. But there are limits to the ways in which these changes occur. The problem raised at the beginning of this section – if there is no 'true' meaning why can't we propose absolutely *any* meaning? – is a problem that actually arises only in practice. In theory, we might accept that we *could* offer any meaning. In practice, however, there are at least some determinate properties of film narratives, and because any audience member is at a particular point in history he or she has a limited set of options through which he or she might view a film. This may not resolve the initial contradiction, but it will enable us to engage in critical practice and examine the ways in which we, as audiences, explore the social and textual potential for meaning within feature films.

SUGGESTIONS FOR FURTHER WORK

1. The body of argument on psychoanalysis and the cinema is large and difficult, but perhaps the most clear and cogent summary of it can be found in Dudley Andrew's *Concepts in Film Theory* (1984). It is not, however, for the faint-hearted. For those seeking more discussion of the subject, the second volume of Nichols's *Movies and Methods* (1985) has some useful and important examples. This volume also contains Laura Mulvey's article, 'Visual pleasure and the narrative cinema', summarized earlier, and a series of feminist responses to it. Further discussions of the female spectator can be found in Deidre Pribram's *Female Spectators* (1988) or in Gamman and Marshment's *The Female Gaze* (1988).
2. For an account of the battle for audiences, and an overview of the structure of the movie business, see Gorham Kindem (ed.) *The American Movie Industry* (1982).
3. It is worth looking at a tradition of audience research which is not yet developed in film studies, but which is burgeoning in television studies – the ethnographic audience interviews and analysis by such researchers as Dorothy Hobson (1982) on *Crossroads* and David Morley's work (1980) on the *Nationwide* audience. In such studies we are reminded of the cultural determinants of textual readings.
4. The move towards multiplexes has changed the cinema-going experience for us. Do you think it has changed other aspects such as the variety of films on offer and the range of tastes accommodated within the one cinema complex? Are there advantages for the cinema audience in the multiplex, or solely advantages to the film producer and exhibitor?
5. The notion that film is a performative medium is one that deserves further thought. When 'set pieces' occur in films they are greeted with affection and pleasure. They are also those moments for which we remember a film. The most memorable moment for most in the audience of *Risky Business* is the half-dressed miming to the Bob Seger song, 'Old-Time Rock 'n' Roll', accomplished with wit and energy by Tom Cruise. It can

stand repeated screenings. Is this kind of moment central to film narratives, do you think? What other examples can you think of? Also, are there actors who specialize in producing such moments? (Eddie Murphy and Robin Williams come to mind here, but there are others.)

6. Examine a promotional campaign for a new film, and see if you can easily detect just what its audience is assumed to be. Then have a look at the film itself and see if this campaign has emphasized one aspect more than another; your task then is to suggest why this has occurred, and if it privileges one 'reading' of the film. This might be a good point to review the notions of meaning canvassed in the last section. Look at a film such as *Point Break* or *Batman Returns*, and see if you can uncover different kinds of readings or addresses to different sections of the audience.

Chapter 6

Film, culture, and ideology

There have been many attempts at understanding the relations between film and culture (or, more accurately, film and ideology). They have occurred under various headings: film and society, film and politics, film and mass culture, for example. Some analyses have focused on the relations between film and trends within popular culture (*Easy Rider* and the hippies of the 1960s, for example), while others have used film as documentary evidence of movements within social history. In many cases, such analyses have assumed a more or less 'reflectionist' relationship between film and society. That is, film is seen as a 'reflection' of the dominant beliefs and values of its culture; if American musicals of the 1940s were Utopian and optimistic, then this must reflect the society's optimism. (An example of such an argument would be Richard Griffith's 'Cycles and genres' (1949).) It should be clear from the rest of this book that such an approach is too primitive; we know, for instance, that American society also produced the alienated and cynical genre of *film noir* during the 1940s: which reflection was the accurate one? The metaphor of reflection is also unsatisfactory because it bypasses the process of selection and combination that goes into the composition of any utterance, whether in film, prose, or conversation. Further, between society and this so-called mirror is interposed a whole set of competing and conflicting cultural, subcultural, industrial, and institutional determinants.

Alternatives to reflectionist views have emerged from structural linguistics, structural anthropology, literary theory, and Marxian theories of ideology. All have contributed to situating the relation between film and society within the broader category of the relationship of representations of *any* kind (photographs, paintings, novels, films) to their culture. Film does not reflect or even record reality; like any other medium of representation it constructs and 're-presents' its pictures of reality by way of the codes, conventions, myths, and ideologies of its culture as well as by way of the specific signifying practices of the medium. Just as film works *on* the meaning systems of culture – to renew, reproduce, or review them – it is also produced *by* those meaning systems. The film-maker, like the novelist or the story-teller, is a *bricoleur* – a sort of handyman who does the best s/he can with the materials at hand. The film-maker uses the representational conventions and repertoires available within the culture in order to make something fresh but familiar, new but generic, individual but representative.

The result of cultural approaches to 'film as representation' is ultimately to focus on the relations between film's representational 'languages' and ideology. Nevertheless, before dealing with this, we need to fill out the overview further. There are two broad categories of culturalist approach to the relation between film and culture: textual and contextual. The textual approach focuses on the film text, or a body of film texts, and 'reads' from them information about the cultural function of film. For example, Andrew Tudor's work on film movements (1974) is text-based; his initial premise is that the texts of German expressionism or Italian neo-realism have something in common which can be understood as expressions of particular aspects of those cultures. We can read, for instance, the recurrence of father–son conflicts in the plots of German expressionist films as symbolic representations of the deep political split between the old and the new guard in the Weimar Republic.

Genre criticism is also initially text-based, even though it may attempt to trace changes in genres to their sources within the culture producing them. Will Wright's study of the western, discussed in Chapter 4, follows such a pattern, as does Schrader's work (1972) on *film noir*, or Dyer's work (1977) on the musical. In general, these textual approaches are responding to a set of conclusions about the specific characteristics of the film text(s); then, operating on the assumption of the culture's 'authorship' of the text, they trace the myths or ideologies of the films back to their sources within the culture. So the suspicion of women in *film noir* is traced back to a series of 'causes', and the Utopian myths which structure musicals are outlined in some detail. Often there is a strong structuralist impulse in such work, since the similarities between films are emphasized more than the differences, and the tendency is to work with many 'typical' texts rather than a few 'individualized' texts.

Although there is no hard distinction between the two angles of approach, contextual approaches analyse the cultural, political, institutional, industrial determinants of – most often – a national film industry. And although there is, again, an interest in film movements which implies a pre-eminent interest in a particular group of film texts, this is not the primary concern of such approaches. It is the process of cultural production rather than the work of representation that concerns these studies. Such work as that of Kristin Thompson or Douglas Gomery in America, John Ellis and Charles Barr in the UK, and John Tulloch and Tom O'Regan in Australia, examines the function of cultural policy, government intervention, censorship, technologies, patterns of ownership within the chain of production–distribution–exhibition, commercial practices within the film industry, public institutions, global aspects of the film industry, and many other factors which affect the textual form of a film (indeed, whether a project *becomes* a film) well before it is ever seen by a critic. Such work often draws on a well-developed tradition in media studies where detailed histories of a TV programme's production and reception are now relatively commonplace. The strong, if now unfashionable, tradition of film history – essentially the proposition of an aesthetic 'great tradition' for the cinema – has now been hijacked (by, for instance, Douglas Gomery) to explore film's industrial history. This has been increasingly useful in developing an understanding of film and culture.

The combination of these two approaches – textual and contextual – has enormous explanatory power. (In the USA, Bordwell, Steiger, and Thompson's *The Classical Hollywood Cinema* (1985) and in Australia, Susan Dermody and Elizabeth Jacka's two-volume cultural history of the revival, *The Screening of Australia* (1987), have demonstrated this.) The combination is also very unwieldy. It is simply beyond our capacity to deal with all the determinants necessary to understand fully the cultural relationships which obtain at any particular point in film's history. For this reason, most discussion has focused on the structure, or the theoretical composition, of the relationships. Even the primarily historical accounts are valuable for what they tell us of the structure of the film/culture relationship. The common thread, however, which links the textual and the contextual and makes an understanding of them complementary rather than mutually exclusive, is that both industry and text, the processes of production and of reception, must be in some way related to ideologies.

The term 'ideology' is itself continually being redefined, contested, and explored within all areas of cultural theory. There is no incontestable definition of ideology. Put at its simplest, we can say that implicit in every culture is a 'theory of reality' which motivates its ordering of that reality into good and bad, right and wrong, them and us, and so on. For this 'theory of reality' actually to work as a structuring principle it needs to be unspoken, invisible, a property of the natural world rather than human interests. Ideology is the term used to describe the system of beliefs and practices that is produced by this theory of reality; and although ideology itself has no material form, we can see its material effects in all social and political formations, from class structure to gender relations to our idea of what constitutes an individual. The term is also used to describe the workings of language and representation within culture which enable such formations to be constructed as 'natural'.

The culture's ideological system is not monolithic but is composed of competing and conflicting classes and interests, all fighting for dominance. The process is, in a sense, replicated in our narratives. In Chapter 4, I used Lévi-Strauss to suggest that narratives set up binary oppositions which are resolved at their end; it was further suggested that the oppositions themselves were composed of representations of competing ideological positions. (I discussed how *Desperately Seeking Susan* explores opposing definitions of marriage, femaleness, and sexuality through the contrasting lifestyles of Roberta and Susan.) If our narratives do work to resolve social contradictions symbolically, what they must deal with are those existing political divisions or inequities between groups, classes, or genders which have been constructed as natural or inevitable within our societies. Films, then, both as systems of representation and as narrative structures, are rich sites for ideological analysis.

Although cultural studies have produced a welter of ideological analyses of film texts (which 'read off' the ideology from the text), it is important to stress that ideologies structure institutions as well as texts. Our legal system, for instance, is biased towards the defence of property. Although the crime of murder suffers the maximum penalty in most western countries, in general it is true to say that offences such as arson and theft are treated more severely than assault or, until relatively recently, rape. This, we might say, is 'simply historical'. Yet history is constructed too; it is the selection and combination of events, sequences, causes, and effects. (We might say that history has a history.) Ideology works to obscure the process of history so that it appears natural, a process we cannot control and which it seems churlish to question. Yet history is the product of competing interests, all attempting to centre their own interests as those of the nation. The history of the institutions of the law reveals discrimination against the poor; the bias towards the protection of property clearly favours those who have most property – presumably, the propertied classes who framed the laws. Yet the institution of the law is normally seen to be above class, above ideology, above politics.

Film institutions have political interests which ultimately determine what films are made, let alone what films are seen. The examination of the operation of these institutions reveals the nature of the interests they serve, the objectives they pursue, and what their function means for the audiences, the industry, and the culture as a whole.

Considerations of the workings of ideology are relevant to both kinds of cultural approach – the textual and the contextual. I wish to stay with this contextual approach for the moment, in order to look, first, at how a film industry participates in the construction of the 'nation'. The second step is to examine this area of cultural production through an illustrative case, surveying the forces determining the development of the Australian film industry during the revival of the 1970s.

FILM AND NATIONAL CULTURE

The idea that the nation-state is the natural form of political organization is a relatively modern one. Nevertheless, most people these days expect our membership of the nation to bind us together, enabling us to achieve more than we could as separate cells or groups of interests. Identification with the nation is often a source of pride and pleasure, too; sporting events, national celebrations of coronations, inaugurations, or holidays such as Independence Day or Anzac Day, are important and satisfying rituals of cultural membership. But we also know that identifications with 'the nation' can be extremely arbitrary. Post-war reconstructions of European national boundaries were clearly arbitrary and cannot have hoped to construct 'national' allegiances easily with a line drawn across a map. Recent events have revealed how unsatisfactory such strategies have been. The Middle East is a further site of the rejection of what are seen as arbitrary attempts to establish definitions of separate nations. This may be an extreme example, but one could also ask whether the Welsh or the Scottish internalize the same idea of the 'nation' as the residents of England. Are Australian Aborigines part of the Australian 'nation', despite their relative powerlessness and subordination? Are the differences between San Francisco, California, and Montgomery, Alabama, more substantial than the similarities?

Opponents of nationalism see it as a dangerously effective tool of persuasion; to accept that the good of the nation is pre-eminent is also to accept the possibility of subordination to that good. To accept the possibility is, sooner or later, to experience the reality. So there are at least two sides to nationalism; it can be a positive political benefit or a real political danger. On the one hand, the idea of the nation is one way of mobilizing the sense of identity without which no social group can survive; the rituals of the nation allow us to celebrate and confirm our membership. On the other hand, it can be used to convince those who are inequitably treated to accept their subordination as being in the national interest. When Dr Johnson said that patriotism was the last refuge of the scoundrel, he referred to the persuasive power unleashed by the invocation of the nation. It is very difficult to place your own interests above those of the nation without seeming to be selfish and unprincipled. Most importantly, the idea of the nation can operate at the most basic levels of meaning and discourse. It becomes an overriding set of priorities which define what is acceptable and what is not, what is normal and what is not, all through defining what is Australian (or British or American) and what is not.

Identification with the nation is an essential prerequisite for political power. We can see the political parties at election time scramble to identify themselves with the flag, with national values, or with the signifiers of an 'essence' of the nation – be it a colonial war in South America, a 12-metre yacht called *Australia II*, or a group of astronauts. Political parties attempt to centre themselves as representative of the nation; by so doing they hope to convince voters that their interests, the nation's interests, and the voters' interests (as members of the nation) are identical. In wider conceptions of politics – that is, not party politics but power relations generally – the idea of the nation is enlisted in achieving and maintaining hegemony. Hegemony is the process by which members of society are persuaded to acquiesce in their own subordination, to abdicate cultural leadership in favour of sets of interests which are represented as identical, but may actually be antithetical, to their own. The subordinated are persuaded by the ideologies on offer rather than the particulars of their material conditions (which might be the practical result of such ideologies). Hegemony's aim is to resist social change and maintain the status quo.

The regulation and control of definitions of art, of literature, and of the national film industry are also hegemonic in that the imperative is always to restrict and limit the proliferation of representations of the nation. (This is because the proliferation of representations also proliferates different definitions.) Representations of the nation are themselves particularly important since they both produce and reproduce the dominant points of view. This does not mean that we only have one version of the nation – although ideally that is what hegemony could mean. What is does mean is that the various representations will enjoy a different status and will have different meanings. In effect, they will construct a different nation. So the British culture constructed in *Chariots of Fire* is different to the British culture constructed in *The Long Good Friday*. Similarly, if the star is the 'type of the individual' within the culture, the face of Anthony Andrews will represent a very different type of the individual to the face of Bob Hoskins. Such differences can be contradictory and therefore threatening; in such cases, the cultural institutions might attempt to limit or control the multiplicity of representations by depicting some as marginal or crass, for instance. But this strategy may be actively inhibited by the audience's thirst for variety and their active toleration of differences. As we shall see in the Australian example, the pressure for hegemony is often met by the resistance of the popular, 'unofficial', culture.

Like other ideological constructions, representations of the nation are not 'fixed'; their political and cultural importance is such that they are sites of considerable competition. To gain control of the representational agenda for the nation is to gain considerable power over individuals' view of themselves and each other. This is one of the reasons why there is so much concern within so many countries over the domination of film and television production and distribution by the United States of America. If we understand our world (or our nation) through its representations, foreign control of the major media of representation does threaten the coherence of the individual's understanding of that world (or nation). The American domination of the mass media has, to some extent, normalized American images of society. Residents of Australia have only recently come to accept Australian urban images for their cinema screens and, only a little less recently, Australian accents in advertising, and radio or television announcers. The cultural hegemony facilitated by this domination of the mass media has worried many countries, and not only on behalf of their media industries.

There is a degree of exaggeration here that can imply greater cultural/national differences than actually exist; the withdrawal of all American films would not remove all evidence of sexism from Australian cinemas, nor the incidence of cultural chauvinism in British cinemas. However, film does serve important cultural functions and those countries which have set up their own industries aim at recovering some control over these functions. They can at least break the silence often maintained about their own culture within American cinema. For Britain, Australia, Canada, New Zealand, and many Scandinavian, South American, and European countries, the question for the last forty years has not been 'should we have a national cinema?' but 'what kind of cinema should it be?' Despite the fact that the mainstream feature film is a global industry, and that even the most successful of the national industries are still enclosed within the macro-structures of the American industry, the ideological power of film has been recognized in these competing, if subordinated, voices of national film industries.

In general, the results of this development have been twofold. Firstly, most countries have set up a network of institutions or government policies to control foreign input and encourage indigenous output. Measures taken include box-office levies (Sweden), income tax incentives for investors (Australia), maximum quotas on foreign films (Britain), and limitations on vertical integration with multinational companies. The more positive moves include the establishment of a film and television school

(Australia), national film-financing bodies (Canada), grants and subsidies (Britain), and government-funded marketing enterprises of the kind that Britain and Australia have mounted at the annual international market-place of Cannes. The 'nationalization' of film promotion through such national marketing offices reveals how closely indigenous film production is connected to the representation and dissemination of images of the nation at home and overseas. What we see is not just a commercial enterprise, but a national cultural project (or projection) as well.

This introduces the second aspect. When films act as *representatives* of as well as *representations* of the nation overseas they become subject to a different regime of inspection. They are assessed, for instance, for their appropriateness as tourist advertisements, or for their 'typicality' as depictions of national life. (This is not something that tends to happen to American films, however.) The ways in which the texts produced by the national industries are patrolled for their images, for their suitability as the national 'touring team', offer another set of determinants of what is produced, what is distributed, and what is positively received by audiences and by critics. And although we are not talking about American mainstream cinema now, it is in such texts and in their conditions of production that we can most clearly see the relationship between film, culture, and ideology. The lessons learnt from such texts and such conditions can easily be applied to any national cinema, including the American cinema.

This brings us full circle, from the context of national cultural production to the film texts themselves. As I said earlier, one cannot hope to do more than chart the intersection of the forces and conditions of film production and reception. But it is illustrative to look at one relatively self-contained example for the lessons it carries about the processes of cultural production. This example is the revival of the Australian film industry, its recovery from near-extinction during the 1970s.

A NATIONAL CINEMA: THE AUSTRALIAN REVIVAL

Australia was one of the early participants in the development of a film industry. An Australian Salvation Army film, *Soldiers of the Cross* (1901), has some claim to being the first full-length feature in the world, although it was not a continuous film but a mixture of slides, film, music, and the spoken word. *The Story of the Kelly Gang* (1906) has slightly stronger claims to being the longest narrative film to that date in the world. Whatever the validity of such claims, Australian film-makers responded quickly to overseas developments and for the first twenty years of this century enjoyed significant local success. However, increasingly during the 1920s and certainly with the arrival of sound, the industry languished. The professional quality of the local films gradually declined, vertical integration of the industry froze out all but British and American imports, and by the end of the Second World War Australia had lost its last feature production company. For the next twenty years almost without exception, Australia was a cheap location for foreign productions (*On the Beach*), British or American co-productions of Australian stories (*The Sundowners* and *Smiley*), and the occasional brave attempt to revive the Australian feature (*Three in One*). Attempts to keep feature production alive dwindled into an attempt to keep the local newsreel industry alive, but when television arrived in 1956 even the newsreel began to disappear.

It is worth noting that encapsulated accounts like the one above make historical processes sound inevitable. They are not, and the failure of the various Australian governments to protect their film industry from foreign competition, or from the discriminatory practices of foreign-owned exhibition and distribution chains, is part of cinema history in Australia, as it is in Britain. However, during the first half of the 1960s, some interest was expressed at government level in determining if a film industry would be viable in Australia. History can be changed, if those in power can be convinced that the change is in their interests. The arrival of TV in Australia had highlighted the need for the policing of foreign content on Australian screens, as well as revealing the importance of a film industry in supplying the infrastructure and the work force for developments in TV and theatrical drama. Both areas were just beginning to grow at the time. The film industry also had considerable potential as a feeder industry, supplying work to a wide range of arts-related occupations – writers, set designers, graphic designers, actors, sound engineers, script editors, camera operators, and many others. As Australia had restricted the use of foreign advertisements on television – commercials shown in Australia had to be made by Australians – a small film industry had grown up within the advertising sector. Peter Weir (*Picnic at*

16   The Australian version of the poster for Peter Weir's *Gallipoli*. In America, the slogan read 'from a place you've never heard of, comes a story you'll never forget' (courtesy, Associated R & R Films)

Hanging Rock, *Witness*) and Fred Schepisi (*Jimmie Blacksmith*, *Plenty*) are among the directors who worked on advertisements, even well into the 1980s. The potential of this group was clearly not exhausted by working on commercials. There were, then, many industrial and economic arguments which suggested that an expanded Australian film industry would benefit existing and related industries. By the end of the 1960s, these arguments were reinforced by another factor: an increasingly powerful nationalist mythology that came to see film as the most desirable medium for projecting an image of the new confidence and maturity seen to mark contemporary Australian culture and society.

In 1969, there were no feature film production companies operating permanently in Australia; there was no film financing from government sources outside the documentary unit, the Commonwealth Film Unit (later called Film Australia); and drama production for Australian TV was very limited. Fully equipped studios such as that of Artransa in Sydney survived by shooting advertisements. There was still resistance to Australian images and voices in the media. It was only in 1967 (eleven years after TV arrived) that Australian-made TV programmes finally dominated the top ten rating programmes for the year. In this context, and as a result of several government inquiries and reports as well as the personal lobbying of the Prime Minister of the day, John Gorton, the government made its first major intervention to encourage Australian film production.

Between 1969 and 1971 a film-financing institution was set up (the Australian Film Development Commission), a training institution was established (the Australian Film and Television School), and a range of other concessions and incentives were introduced to encourage local production. The boost to local production highlighted the problems that Australian films experienced in winning distribution and exhibition. At the time, there were two major distributors in the country, Hoyts and Greater Union – neither of them Australian-owned. An investigation by the Tariff Board – set up to protect local industries from 'unfair' competition – made threatening noises about the need to limit foreign ownership and break up distribution monopolies. As a result of such pressure, a minor distributor, Roadshow, which was primarily Australian-owned, took a more supportive attitude towards the Australian product. However, even Roadshow was dependent upon overseas films (it distributed for Warner Bros), so there was a limit to the help it cared to give Australian films by placing them in the right theatres at the right times. The problem has never really been resolved; Australia cannot supply the distributors with enough features for them to risk breaking arrangements with the American suppliers. Despite such problems, from 1970 to 1973 a number of films managed to make money at the box-office: *Stork* and *Alvin Purple* were the most prominent.

The institutional structure established between 1969 and 1975 operated as a large cultural bank. Film-makers approached the Australian Film Development Commission (later called the Australian Film Commission) with outlines of their projects. Their suitability, track record, and viability were assessed at this and every subsequent stage. Once the project was favourably assessed, the AFDC/AFC funded further development of the script and the preparation of a budget. Once past this stage, the AFDC/AFC could decide to invest in the project through further seed money, a loan, or a straight grant aimed at completing the film. Apart from exceptional cases such as *The Adventures of Barry McKenzie*, film-makers had to find the majority of their budgets from private sources – even if this meant mortgaging the family home. (These were not yet Hollywood-style budgets, however; *Picnic at Hanging Rock* was made for less than half a million dollars, which was almost double the average budget for Australian films made in that year, 1975. *Towering Inferno*, an American success of the same year, cost US$14 million.) Between 1969 and 1975, the government film institutions (the federal AFC was soon joined by separate state authorities such as the South Australian Film Corporation and Film Victoria) provided as much as 60 per cent of total budgets in some cases, and as little as 20 per cent in others. In the same period, support from the industry itself – that is, the private sector of the television companies and the distribution and exhibition chains – was derisory; it hit a high of 28 per cent of film budgets in 1970 and dropped to a low of 2 per cent in 1973. They were not prepared to gamble. This is highlighted by the dramatic increase in industry investment, up from 4 per cent to 46 per cent in 1975 – the year of the critical successes of *Picnic at Hanging Rock* and *Sunday Too Far Away*.

This structure was occasionally administered in a bizarre and *ad hoc* manner (Dermody and Jacka's book (1987) documents this), but it got the industry under way. The first films to catch the attention of the newly delivered Australian audience were the so-called 'ocker' comedies: *Stork*, *Alvin Purple*, and *The Adventures of Barry McKenzie*. The ocker films represented a masculine, populist, and cheerfully vulgar view of Australian society. Australian social practices and idiosyncrasies were celebrated for their own sake rather than for their contribution to world culture, while beer, sex, and bodily functions figured large in the action. The films depended on a very specific definition of Australian-ness.

It is at this point that we can see the ideology behind the film institutions click into place. Initial support for Australian film talked of making 'frankly commercial films' for a local and overseas market. The ocker films were certainly commercial and at least *Barry McKenzie* was successful in Britain. But the critics and the funding bodies were appalled by them and by their success. The ocker films dashed all hopes of establishing an image of Australia as a land of sophistication equal to the centres of Europe, with a culture of substance. Instead, Australia looked like the kind of place most of the Eurocentric critics and government film assessors would hate to inhabit. The specificity of the films' depiction of contemporary Australian popular culture was an embarrassment to people who had no commitment to it in the first place but had rather hoped to help the nation to transcend it.

In a 1975 report on the industry, the supporting rhetoric underwent a crucial change. What Australia needed was 'quality' films which could be the cultural flagships of the nation. Financial capital was not the object any longer (relatively few Australian films made since the revival have returned significant profits). Cultural capital was now the goal.

Although the government film-financing bodies were never organized enough to be in any way conspiratorial, there was remarkable unanimity about the kinds of films which state and federal film commissions supported over the next five years. Instead of more ocker comedies, we had what Dermody and Jacka (1987) have called the 'AFC genre', a national film style determined by the preferences of the funding bodies and greeted critically as a source of national pride. Representative are such films as *Picnic at Hanging Rock* – visually stylish, low-key, highly aestheticized period dramas which offered the visual exoticism of the Australian scenery coupled with moderately symbolic and open-ended narrative forms. Australia was caught in the amber of its history, its present credentials implied by the style and sensibility of its representation of its past. These films deferred to European standards of cinematic taste – the models were the French *nouvelle vague* and the BBC historical TV drama – rather than to American objectives of entertainment. Beautiful and untroubling films, they were politically conservative and, despite the obsession with history, they said little about contemporary Australia. In the years 1971 to 1977, out of eighty-seven features made, less than ten (if we exclude the ocker comedies) dealt with contemporary Australian society with any degree of seriousness. The obsession with historical drama seemed designed to establish that Australia *had* a history and therefore *was* a culture. Formally, films which moved outside the boundaries of the AFC genre and into Hollywood genres – action or adventure, for instance – were reviled by the critics and spurned by the government institutions (although they did pull in the audiences). *Mad Max* is relatively unusual for its time because it was made with no government support at all.

It is hard not to see the 'screening of Australia' as a complex exercise involving not only the screening of an image on film, but also a 'screening out' of certain kinds of films; those selected were European in their aesthetic assumptions and constructed Australian-ness through landscape or history rather than through popular cultural forms. In the AFC Genre there was a deep ideological resistance to contemporary representations of the nation, perhaps because they almost inevitably celebrated indigenous cultural formations.

It is true that these patterns become less pronounced after 1977. Changes in the funding policies increased film-makers' reliance on private backing, and changes in the tax laws offered substantial incentives (at least until 1987) for investors to use film as a means of writing off high tax liabilities. Further, the designation of film as the cultural flagship slackened its hold as the potential of the TV mini-series became apparent. The American success of the Australian mini-series *A Town Like Alice* alerted even the most Eurocentric to the possibilities of the US market and hastened the application of film-funding guidelines to TV production from which they had hitherto been excluded. Now, TV productions can attract government finance in the same way as film, and TV drama production is seen to be a more commercial option than the feature film. Predictably enough, during the 1980s history repeated itself, as a parade of AFC Genre historical mini-series swept across the nation's TV screens, albeit in competition with the tougher, more critical productions such as Kennedy-Miller's stylish *Vietnam*.

Film critics outside Australia have talked of the Australian revival as a movement with recognizable stylistic characteristics. These characteristics are not just the quirks of certain film-makers, fortuitously working in the same industry at the same time. They are the results of a number of textual and contextual determinants. The dominance of an aesthetic visual style is produced by the ideology of the AFC and other film commissions (and, in turn, the governments overseeing their funding) who saw in it a signification of the sophistication of the culture; such assumptions are nicely overturned when it is noted that the specific performance within that style could be traced to the early training of cinematographers like Russell Boyd in television advertising. The open-ended narratives emerge from a narrative tradition in Australian prose (see Turner (1986) for an account of this) that is inconclusive and ambiguous, a fashionable interest in *nouvelle vague* existentialism, and the anti-individualist strategy of deferring any ideological narrative resolution on to history. (Many of the films just finish rather than 'end', and seal over this unsatisfying conclusion by the use of historical subtitles, summarizing characters' subsequent fates.) Government intervention in the industry had always constructed the films as cultural products, representing Australia as directly as its career diplomats. The films of this period are almost 'official' in their relation to Australian culture, and the vibrant iconoclasm of the ocker films would have enlivened many of them. The specific texts, then, emerge as the results of complex negotiations between industry, institutions, and national culture, and express a range of accepted ideological definitions of Australia. So the critics approved *Gallipoli*, with its hazy mythologizing of Australian soldiers as innocent and displaced, but decent and robust, descendants from European traditions; but *Crocodile Dundee*'s construction of the shrewd, potentially criminal (but basically decent), populist proved unacceptable.

While some countries might envy the level of government support given to Australian film during the 1970s – and only the American industry can survive without such support – it is as well to remember that this also binds the industry back into the nation and its representatives. It is ironic to note that as government support became less important to the Australian film industry, and the influence of private investment stronger, the variety of

Australian films being made widened to range from the low-budget art film of Paul Cox's *Cactus* to the slyly engaging mainstream fare of *Crocodile Dundee*. The latter is the most successful Australian film to date in financial terms, taking over $100 million in America in 1986–7. Together with the *Mad Max* films and *The Man from Snowy River*, it also gives the lie to the conventional wisdom of the 1970s that it is only Hollywood, rather than the subordinate industries, that can make genre films.

Since 1988, there has been a further change in the funding structure which again binds producers back into governmental agendas. In an eery replay of the beginnings of the revival, the 'frankly commercial' rubric has been implicitly revived in the requirement that films seeking support from the new film bank (the Film Finance Corporation) find most of their budget from private sources. The tax concessions used to attract private investment earlier in the 1980s have been wound back to the point where they no longer serve a useful function. The effect of this structural change has been to privilege the clearly commercial project with a good likelihood of TV sales over the more idiosyncratic feature film. As a result, fewer features are now being made, TV mini-series have become prohibitively expensive unless likely to achieve major sales overseas, and the level of confidence in the industry is reflecting the uncertainties around its future.

Despite these structural changes, however, and despite these uncertainties, the familiar battles continue for control over the forms and images found within the Australian films that *are* made. The success of *Crocodile Dundee* provoked precisely the same responses that greeted the ocker films. Is this an appropriate image of Australia? Is it art? Is it Australian? Should governments spend money on this kind of thing? None of these are the real questions. They reflect the failure of the institutions to achieve their ideological objectives and they are simply strategies in the battle to regain a measure of regulation and control over the images and the narratives which represent Australia. We should not forget that this, along with the production of these images and narratives, is the business of a national cinema.

IDEOLOGY IN THE TEXT

From the Australian example we can see that arguments about the aesthetic qualities of specific film texts are never objective or disinterested. Both the production and reception of film are framed by ideological interests, no matter how insistently this might be denied. In this section, I want to examine the workings of ideology in the film text itself. The starting-point is the simple one that ideology is read from film texts, consciously or unconsciously, and the relationship between each text and its culture is traceable to ideological roots.

The problem, however, is how to deal with this. It is impossible to stand outside ideology and talk about it in a language which is itself free of ideology. It is also hard to see things which we like to think are parts of our identity as ideologically constructed. One's tastes, for instance, are formed through ideology, but it is difficult to accept that something as essential to our sense of ourselves is culturally constructed. Just as the concepts themselves can be a little unsettling, ideological textual analysis can have its moments too. It can be, in turns, dizzyingly complex or ridiculously simple. The next two sections – without falling into either of these extreme categories, it is to be hoped – will outline some of the basic assumptions and applications of this mode of representational analysis.

More than any others, ideological considerations allow us to begin to understand the relationship between film texts and their cultural contexts. Importantly, ideological approaches reject the view of the film text as 'unitary' in meaning; that is, as making only one kind of sense, without contradictions, exceptions, or variations in the interpretations made by different members of the audience. Rather, the text is a kind of battleground for competing and often contradictory positions. Of course, this competition usually results in a victory for the culture's dominant positions, but not without leaving cracks or divisions through which we can see the consensualizing work of ideology exposed. Through such cracks, ideological analysis provides the point of entry to an understanding of the film's formal process of construction. These cracks, or gaps, in the text are not simply the inventions of the critic. They are often points where the audience is aware of a weakness in the narrative: where a union between lovers is formed that is 'unconvincing' or where the death of a character might seem unmotivated or arbitrary, or where one might have expected the ending to have a different emotional inflection. Often the formal problems we might discern within a film are traceable to the intransigence of the ideological opposition; an unsatisfactory

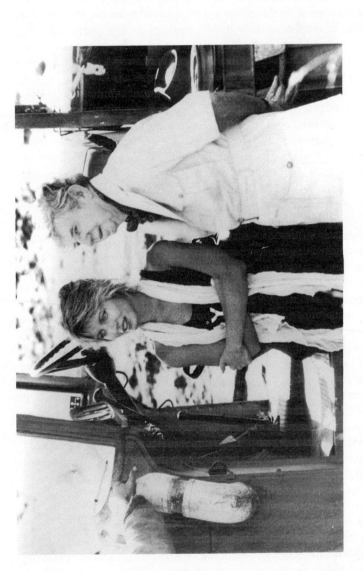

17 Linda Kozlowski (Sue Charlton) and John Meillon (Wally Reilly) in a scene from *Crocodile Dundee* (used with permission, courtesy Kakanda Pty Ltd)

ending in a film may emerge from the failure to unite the ideological alternatives convincingly.

As the above paragraphs might suggest, generalization is risky in this area. Ideology is a slippery concept since it is not an abstract entity which can be described separately from its workings in a specific act of signification. So we will move to the discussion of an example – a film which highlights the complexities of the working of ideology because it was seen to be explicitly ideological by members of its audience but not by its makers. Fritz Lang's *Metropolis* reveals how unconsciously ideology can work and how it can live in the formal properties of the individual film text.

In 1927, German expressionism was a greatly respected film movement, marked by a strong visual style which employed low-key lighting, geometric shapes, oblique camera angles, and sharp juxtapositions of light and dark. Its narratives were melodramatic, offering Gothic and supernatural plots as often as contemporary stories. At the time, the Weimar Republic of Germany was in political disarray, suffering the trauma of defeat in the First World War and the uncertainty of continual changes in government (fifteen different administrations from the beginning of the Weimar Republic until the election of Hitler's National Socialists), and lacking any one political grouping capable of presiding over the reconstruction of the national identity, while a plethora of groups was singled out for special blame and fear: the 'international Jewish conspiracy', the Communists, the dying aristocracy, even the Weimar itself. The film-makers were relatively aloof from this, however, and there are remarkably few direct references to German domestic politics in expressionist films.

It was in this climate that *Metropolis* was made. The film tells the story of a workers' revolution in a futuristic dictatorship. The revolution is actually instigated through a plot hatched between the ruler of Metropolis and a mad scientist, and is intended to discredit a workers' liberation movement which is given the contradictory attributes of both Christianity and Communism. The workers destroy the factory and flood their homes, but stability is reinstated by the end of the film. The ruler's son mediates between the workers and the boss, as Christ mediates between God and Man. Or, as the film has it, he is the 'heart' which guides the co-operation between the 'head' (the ruler) and the 'hands' (the workers). Although the film establishes the oppression of the workers, its final frames show them surrendering their power to a newly humanized ruler.

Lang was not an overtly political film-maker at this point, and certainly had no special admiration for Nazism; he saw the film, as he said later, as a rather 'silly' melodrama. Hitler, however, saw it differently and admired its dramatization of Fascist philosophy. In fact, Hitler was so impressed with Lang, a Jew, that he offered him the post of head of the German film industry and the status of 'honorary Aryan'. Lang, to his credit, fled Nazi Germany for America where he became known for, among other things, his anti-Nazi films during the Second World War.

Ideology is unconscious, as Lang's history demonstrates. He was not a Nazi, nor was he pro-Nazi. Yet his film brought Hitler great satisfaction. This is because Lang, the film-maker/*bricoleur*, used what the culture made available to him – not only its languages but its meanings. These included the dominant images of power as patriarchal, fatherly, and the assumption that political unrest was always undesirable and that reformist politics were either messianic or Marxist. The pentangle (five-pointed star) used to represent the evil of the scientist Rotwang, with its close similarity to the star of David, invokes anti-Semitism. The film's view of the people as gullible and to be saved from themselves is probably also traceable to cultural roots. Most of these assumptions and meanings were appropriated by Nazism as well as by Lang's film. Fritz Lang was not the 'author' of the discourses of *Metropolis*; his culture was.

The ideology of a film does not take the form of direct statements or reflections on the culture. It lies in the narrative structure and in the discourses employed – the images, myths, conventions, and visual styles. Even though *Metropolis* is a conventional melodrama involving a love affair between an individualized hero and heroine, it is not a film which is about character or even about plot. Its most obvious attribute is its portrait of a world. The film's distinctiveness and power arise from its opening series of representations of dehumanizing working conditions, the physical design of the future world, and the depiction of a rigidly hierarchized physical environment in which the people live. These aspects of the film are both prescient and striking. For the contemporary viewer at least, who may find the love interest a little dated, they are the discourses of a pre-eminently social, political film.

This being the case, the ending of the film needs to resolve its social/political conflicts as well as its personal dilemmas – but it

18   The art direction and set design for *Metropolis* still impresses. Ridley Scott's *Blade Runner*, almost sixty years later, owes explicit debts to it (courtesy of the National Film and Sound Archive of Australia)

does not. It is characteristic of the workings of ideology that they express social or political differences as personal and individual, therefore to be resolved at the personal not the political level, and a sign of *individual* weakness, not the weakness of the social or political *system*. The ending of *Metropolis* resolves the love interest, reunites the father and son, but changes almost nothing in the social or political structure of its world. The powerful early scenes of dehumanized workers being sacrificed to the machines are cancelled out by the workers' capitulation to what is a corrupt and irresponsible deployment of power. By the end, the power of the masses is represented as the real threat, and this legitimates the reinstatement of the fatherly, benevolent dictatorship. The masses need protection from themselves, it seems, and the guardianship of their future is placed safely in the hands of the ruler of Metropolis.

The film is composed of a series of moves and counter-moves which are not only narratively but also ideologically motivated. Its opening images explicitly connect totalitarianism with capitalism by making the Master of Metropolis an industrialist. However, the socialist alternatives inevitably invoked are not supported. The robot-Maria is used as a metaphor for the temptress of revolutionary Communism and her demonic destructiveness articulates a warning against such temptations. The destruction she causes legitimates the need for a restraining power, for a 'head' who can control the 'hands'. When the Master undergoes a humanizing change of heart, his rule is again benevolent, paternal. This is the only concession required to make the workers surrender their destructive power back to the state. The film is marked by a deep formal and ideological contradiction: the powerful image of the working class as victims is reversed into an image of the working class as agents of their own destruction; or to put it another way, the critique of class domination and capitalism is overcome by a dread of Communism specifically, and generally of uncontrolled social change.

Contemporary audiences certainly find this unsatisfying, as the contradictions are crudely smoothed over with the invocation of loyalty to the father, and his reciprocal love for his people. It is this latter aspect, presumably, which appealed to Hitler – the binding of the group back into the nation, the investment of faith in the mother/father, as well as the melodramatic depictions of alternative political positions.

In order to deal with the film's ideology we have to deal, even in this preliminary way, with the surfaces of the text, the formal systems of signification. (In so doing we have uncovered at least two opposing readings, two sets of signification which might make sense of it for an audience.) The method of analysis drives us further than one might expect into the construction of the text, given that the objective of the analysis is ultimately to move *from* the text back to the culture which produced it.

The final point, before leaving this example, is to qualify one false impression that it may have given. I have already talked of the notion of hegemony. This account of *Metropolis* may imply that hegemonic systems are comprehensively, inevitably, controlling and determining. This is misleading. Films must take on some relation to ideologies but they do not necessarily recycle them. John Ellis (1982: 74) approaches this point in the following way:

> General ideological notions are assumed by narrative films. These assumptions are established through repetition, a characteristic of ideological reproduction which leads us to assume things unless they are specifically contradicted. Yet mere repetition alone is not the characteristic of the film text. It may take for granted certain meanings, certain assumptions, but it exists to take risks, to work through ideological problems. Hence the innovatory character of the film in relation to ideological meanings. They are not reproduced so much as refreshed, not so much repeated as reworked.

I would go further, and say that they may actively oppose or subvert dominant meanings. For example, in the Australian ocker films a popular narrative form carries meanings that are subversive of some dominant patterns. The result was that such films were critically squashed, but they did get made and they did find their audiences.

It is important to see the dynamic nature of ideology. Although culture is subjected to hegemonic constructions, this is a process – not a permanently achieved state. The constellations of hegemonic interests can change. The constituent ideologies can change too. As I suggested earlier, we can see the process being acted out in narrative films where ideologies confront each other as structural opposites in the narrative itself – as good guy and bad guy, as right move and wrong move – to be resolved in the final reel. The film's closure mimics the individual processes of making decisions, taking positions, and making sense of the experiences that we go through every day of our lives.

ISSUES IN IDEOLOGICAL ANALYSIS

Although it is important to retain a sense of the heterogeneity of the ideological system, the vast majority of the work on film and ideology has concentrated on the ways in which film texts inevitably support existing social conditions, and accept existing explanations of those social conditions. Although the constitution of the ruling interests within culture does change, the function of hegemony does not; it works to maintain the status quo. In film studies, this has provoked élitist critiques of the medium from one side of the argument, but more often it provokes analysis which is aimed at revealing ideologies operating in film and in the culture. Study of ideology in film provides an insight into the meaning systems of the culture and into the ways in which such systems are inscribed into all kinds of social practice.

One target of such studies is the kind of film which seems to be critical of dominant positions – feminist films, for instance, or a film like *Platoon* which appears to attack US involvement in Vietnam. *Tootsie* could be seen as having some progressive attributes; it depicts a man experiencing the sexism normally handed out to women. He learns just how difficult men make women's lives. In his persona as Dorothy, Mike Dorsey (Dustin Hoffman) attempts to 'liberate' his/her female comrades in the television production company, and ultimately leads the way towards redressing the balance to some extent. On the face of it this might seem to overturn the ideological privileges the male has enjoyed. However, as Judith Williamson (1987) has suggested, this is not necessarily true. Mike Dorsey is still a man even when he pretends to be Dorothy, and the lesson we learn from the film is that men are better at being feminists than women, as well as being better at everything else!

The point of such criticism is to show how potentially critical positions can be articulated within the boundaries of ideology, but are eventually 'clawed back' into the dominant systems to generate their meanings. The first half of the Australian film *Gallipoli* attacks the rich seam of mythology and cultural chauvinism which surrounds the legend of the Anzac (Australian and New Zealand Army Corps) troops' engagement at Gallipoli during the First

World War. The effect of any attack on this legend is to demytho-logize the Anzac heroes, to claim specifically that they were naïve or were duped or misled. *Gallipoli* stops short of carrying this claim through. The second half of the film turns its characters into heroes, as the standard mythologizing framework claws back their individuality and oppositional potential into the conventional legend. The freeze frame at the end of the film – which catches the more idealistic hero at the point of being shot while charging the Turkish trenches – is the filmic equivalent of the commemora-tive statues of the soldier erected in small towns all over Australia after the war. Its ideology is the same, too.

The demands of the narrative – the relentless movement for-ward towards resolution – can serve ideological imperatives too. Moral, political, and social complexities are easily obscured within the tide of narrative. In *Midnight Express*, the death of the sadistic gaoler is preceded by the hero's alibi, the attempted homosexual rape. There is no motivation provided for this rape, other than the guard's specific foreignness. The employment of racist depictions of the prison warders and their attitudes to the prisoners are key determinants of our fear and anger as we watch the film. The death of Sergeant Barnes in *Platoon* is also seen as a kind of rough justice, legitimated by his callous attempt on the life of the Christ-like Sergeant Elias. Yet he is probably more important in his role as scapegoat for the guilt and confusion that the film builds up around the whole issue of American involvement in Vietnam. Barnes is dehumanized by the war; hence his callousness and hence his dispensability within the narrative. But for the audience, to see Barnes's death as politically cathartic, rather than as essen-tially retributive justice, would be a much more ambiguous plea-sure. The drive of the narrative, however, focusing on Taylor's survival and his ultimate delivery from Vietnam, pushes this prob-lem aside.

It is possible to think of competing readings of films as the product of their ideological, as well as their narrative, outcomes. The end of *Working Girl*, for instance, is signalled by the trium-phal soundtrack as the heroine's attempt to cross the line into an executive role achieves success – an office of her own. The camera pulls back, mythologizing the city in which the heroine is working but also reducing her to the status of one person, one window, among thousands. As the camera pulls even further back we lose sight of her altogether and her story is swallowed up in the spectacle of skyscrapers. As a coda to a moral fable of individualist capitalism (which is one way of seeing the film), this closing shot has a very ambiguous effect since it suggests an opposing view of capitalism – as a dehumanizing and alienating system. The end of *Fatal Attraction*, too, is slightly ambiguous: it can be read as reinforcing the ideologies of the family through the consoling positioning of the family photo in the final frame, or alternately, as using this same photo to call up an ironic critique of the effect of these ideologies in this particular family.

Such problems of interpretation, the way in which a viewer is led through the feature film, feed back into a central issue in ideological analysis, that of realism. Realism has acquired a special meaning within this tradition of film analysis. It refers to the dominant mode of narrative film-making, and certainly the dominant mode within Hollywood cinema. Realist film creates a world which is as recognizable as possible; and audiences understand it by drawing analogies between the world of the film and their own world. They are assisted in this process by the lengths that realist film goes to in order to look like real life. The technologies of film production are hidden, so that techniques which might draw attention to the means of construction are kept to a minimum. Editing is as seamless as possible, the *mise-en-scène* is as dense as that of real life, camera movements tend to keep pace with the movement of the spectator's eyes, and perspective is maintained as if there were but one spectator.

Realism's disguising of the constructed as 'the natural' is a direct parallel to the function of ideology. The power of realist film, however, lies in the efficiency of this disguise, its ability to appear to be an unmediated view of reality. Colin MacCabe (1981) has argued that in realist film, television drama and the novel, there is what he calls a 'hierarchy of discourse'. Realist narratives offer problems, dilemmas, deficiencies to be solved or supplied; the reader or viewer makes his/her way through the narrative gaining knowledge about how this is to occur. At the end, the reader possesses full knowledge, the problems are solved, and there is a sense of a satisfying conclusion. MacCabe argues that realist fictions guide the reader very carefully through one set of discourses – a set of values, a narrator, or the control of the perspectives of the camera – which takes on the role of an authoritative narrator. The authority of the narrative 'tells' the reader what to think, closes off questions, and delivers them to the end of the fiction.

The realist text does not question reality or its constituent conditions. Since the realist text depends on the reader seeing it as reality, it cannot question itself without losing authenticity.

MacCabe has claimed that realist films are incapable of expressing opposition to or criticism of dominant values or beliefs, because they depend on them in order to make sense. Even realist modes which represent themselves as critical of dominant values – the TV docu-dramas like *Days of Hope* or *Boys from the Blackstuff* – have been attacked as simply using history to naturalize social divisions; 'that is the way it is', they are supposed to say, and there is 'little we can do about it'.

This series of proposals needs qualification. The realist debate is a large one, and further reading will bring a greater understanding of it than is possible in this small section. I would like to make the point, however, that realism is a system of signification which still has to work within specific contexts. In Australian film, too, realism signifies historical truth, but until 1977 very few films used it to deal with contemporary historical truths. The first few films to do so dealt with marginalized, repressed sections of the community – unemployed youths or the urban poor, for instance. The social and ideological function of films like *Mouth to Mouth* and *Hard Knocks* seems to me to be critical and progressive because they added to the repertoire of images of Australian society, and complicated that repertoire greatly. One needs to be wary of applying this theory to any film or culture. One cannot simply read off the ideology of a film from its formal characteristics.

Other issues can be followed up in further reading. For example, the comprehensiveness of theories of ideology has worried many people, so that theories of resistance to the ideological through the pleasures of the body have surfaced. Some of these have been referred to in Chapter 5. They also raise important qualifications to the notion of ideology. We need to ask if our pleasure at a car chase on film or our day-to-day experience of physical pleasure is constructed in ideology. We might also need to consider if our conceptions of beauty or style are entirely constructed by culture, or if there is something universal and unchanging about such perceptions. One might understand that beauty is culturally coded while still feeling that it would be impossible to see a tropical island as ugly. Even sexual pleasure may be culturally coded; is sexuality a 'realism' that needs to be interrogated? Further, such questions should concern more than just testing the limits to theories of ideology. The notion of pleasure is still, apart from the important progress made within feminist theory, relatively undeveloped in relation to popular cinema. The residue of aesthetic preferences still affects the kinds of films which get talked about, the kinds of problems seen to be of interest in film studies today. A benefit likely to emerge from a cultural interest in film is a more concerted attempt to understand the pleasures provided by mainstream genre films – from horror films to teen movies. It is not enough to think of them working solely through the pleasures of a ritual confirmation of dominant ideologies.

A final problem. For many who first encounter notions of ideology, the argument that they and their identities are culturally constructed is often interpreted as saying that they are not 'real'. It is difficult to get around the sense that there is some genuine reality out there which ideology prevents us getting at. The trick is to realize that whether that is the case or not is immaterial. Our only access to reality is through its representation. Even as we look at a landscape we do so through cultural filters which actually order what we see. (Early paintings of the Australian landscape make it look just like Europe, its native inhabitants resembling classical statues of Greek and Roman heroes rather than what we now see as the distinctive features of the Aborigines.) Representations of the real world are like any other language system, saturated with ideology. However, this 'real' which culture constructs for us to know and live with is no less material in its effects on our lives and our consciousness. Just because we cannot stand outside our way of seeing the world (to 'see' that way of seeing) does not mean that our relation to the world is in some way false or provisional.

There is no really simple way to state this problem. However, Richard Dyer approached a specific aspect of it in his conclusion to *Stars*. Dealing with the notion that beauty is not inherent, even in film stars, and that pleasure is learned rather than instinctive, even in films, he says: 'while I accept utterly that beauty and pleasure are culturally and historically specific, and in no way escape ideology, nonetheless they are beauty and pleasure and I want to hang on to them in some form or another' (1982: 185).

This is a sensible and instructive reaction to the force of ideology and to the pleasure of film.

SUGGESTIONS FOR FURTHER WORK

1. A good, simple application of theories of ideology to another medium of representation, fine art, is worth searching out. John Berger's *Ways of Seeing* (1972) demonstrates clearly how ideology shapes our view of the world. Much discussion of ideology is extremely complex and jargon-ridden, so this book may help students grappling with the concept. A further text which deals with the topics from another angle is John Fiske's *Introduction to Communication Studies* (1982), a companion volume to this book in the 'Studies in Communication' series. Discussion of ideology is to be found in treatments of popular culture – such as Judith Williamson's *Consuming Passions* (1987) or Rosalind Coward's *Female Desire* (1984) – but ideological analyses of films can be found in Nichols's collections of film theory, *Movies and Methods* (1976; 1985), as well as in journals such as *Screen*, *Jump Cut*, *Film Quarterly*, *Australian Journal of Screen Theory*, *Cultural Studies*, and many others.
2. Testing out your understanding of the concept of ideology on some film texts is a good idea. It might be useful, for instance, to turn back to Chapter 4 and examine the evolution of the western as described by Wright in the light of what you now know about ideology. What changes in ideology underlie this evolution? (In fact, is the term 'evolution' itself indicative of an ideological position – developmental, always improving, rather than cyclical or revolutionary?)
3. The references to the realism debate are brief; anyone who wishes to follow it further – and it is a key debate – can find the most important articles collected in Bennett *et al.*, *Popular Television and Film* (1981).
4. Ideology is revealed by examining those things we take for granted. Look at a film of your choice and see just what it takes for granted – at the level of dress, décor, and design as well as at the level of the motivations of major characters. Looking at the representations of women in, say, westerns of the 1950s, reveals that the ways in which women are taken for granted have changed. Are there other such instances you can recall, where change has revealed the dynamic process of ideology?
5. For a discussion of ideology and the film industry, Steve Neale's *Cinema and Technology* (1985) is useful and relatively accessible for such a difficult subject.

6. For a further group of arguments around the notion of pleasure and ideology, see Rutsky and Wyatt (1990) and Noel King's response (1992).
7. Finally, the reading of ideology in film is an interpretative act. Follow the analyses in the next chapter and try to make use of these methods yourself in interpreting films. It is being done skilfully when it does not reduce the films to their constituent ideologies, and when you find as much that is contradictory and conflicting as you find that is unitary and consoling.

Chapter 7

Applications

Most students of film find that they can follow the arguments supporting the various theoretical approaches to the subject. Many encounter difficulty, however, when they are asked to apply these theories to a specific film which they watch and then have to talk or write about. This is partly due to an exaggerated respect for theory; many assume that if the process takes so much theorizing it must be hard. The process of reading a film is complex, but the complexity lies in our attempts to understand the process, rather than to employ it. Everyone 'reads' films; film studies tries to understand how this is done. An important first step to applying the theoretical approaches developed in this book is to maintain some confidence in one's own point of view on a film. This chapter, however, may assist in taking the next steps.

It is usually the close, 'formal', analysis of a film that appears to be the most arcane and difficult: the extraction of key elements of the narrative or visual style that is so much a staple of film studies' texts and teaching. This chapter presents examples of such close formal analysis in order to demonstrate how it is arrived at. In the first example, an account of the opening scenes of *Butch Cassidy and the Sundance Kid* applies the material on film 'languages' from Chapter 3 and on genre from Chapter 4, incorporates some of the discussion of stars from Chapter 5, and heads towards the ideological concerns of Chapter 6. In the second example, *Desperately Seeking Susan* is subjected to a number of approaches; the analyses proceed from ideas of *mise-en-scène* (Chapter 3), structuralist accounts of narrative (Chapter 4), genre (Chapter 4), audiences (Chapter 5), and ideology (Chapter 6). The intention is to demonstrate what the application of these approaches looks like, and to reveal the kinds of information each approach produces. Finally, these are applications of theory, not full (or even particularly clever) readings of the two films.

BUTCH CASSIDY AND THE SUNDANCE KID

Butch Cassidy and the Sundance Kid opens as a silent movie – sepia-toned, flickering, flaring, and unstable. It depicts the exploits of the Hole in the Wall gang, led by Butch Cassidy and the Sundance Kid; the titles tell us they are all dead now but once 'they ruled the West!' It is not clear if the silent film is a documentary or a dramatic recreation of the gang's activities, but it immediately situates the film in a heroic mode, with the distancing, nostalgic effect of the silent film adding to its mythic dimension. The silent footage introduces and accompanies the credits, occupying the left of the screen while the credits run on the right. In addition to the whirring sound of the silent projector, a simple, nostalgic score establishes the emotional texture of the film. As the credits end, the screen goes to black and the words 'Most of what follows is true' come up. This is to be a western which is about westerns and their mythologies.

The sepia tint and the high contrast between light and dark are maintained for the first two sequences of the narrative. These sequences are specifically contained within the same mythic domain by this device, and many of the meanings of the silent prologue leak into the opening five minutes of the narrative. The prologue is a western within a western, offering us images of the classic 'shoot 'em up' in order to signify the film's self-consciousness and to alert the audience to the degree of participation expected from them. The contrast between the sepia-tinted monochrome stock and the colour-film stock used later on is maintained throughout the film as a contrast between the lost, innocent 'past' of the characters, and the wry, knowing 'present' of the audience. Thematically, the juxtaposition of a historical wild west with the modernity of (even silent) film foreshadows the heroes' plight as they become, more clearly as the film progresses, engaging anachronisms. The choice of film stock, then, and its deployment, have a thematic function as well as a stylistic or tonal effect.

The first shot of the narrative establishes the door of a grand, western bank, and then we zoom into the interior. Immediately we have an extreme close-up of Butch Cassidy/Paul Newman's face;

close-ups of his face will dominate the rest of the sequence. Newman's face is highlighted and attractively modelled by the low-key lighting, which emphasizes the lines of the jaw and the definition of the lips, and which reflects off the famous eyes. The sepia toning is now golden, giving his skin a romantic sheen. Although Butch/Newman is 'casing' the bank, the focus is almost continuously on his face, briefly intercut with shots of bars, locks, doors, alarms, and finally an armed guard. A montage of close-ups of 'CLOSED' signs and grilles and doors being shut over a soundtrack of farewells tells us that the bank is closing for the day. The first break from close-ups is a medium long shot of Newman as he moves out of the door into the afternoon glare. He says to the guard, 'What happened to the old bank, it was beautiful?' 'People kept robbing it,' says the guard. 'Small price to pay for beauty,' says Butch as he walks out into the light, clearly disgruntled; here is a bank which will be impossible to rob. The joke works because it is anachronistic; it depends on the audience having seen enough westerns to know that Butch is 'casing' the bank and to recognize his remark as parodic of the generic conventions. Also, the play between the present and the past in the silent prologue watched by today's audience is repeated and focused in Butch's remark.

The lighting, the tint in the film processing, and the concentration on the star's face (even while the bulk of the information offered relates to the bank), all serve the scene's main objectives. The star's face, as stated in Chapter 5, is itself a spectacle, a source of recognition and pleasure for the audience. In this opening sequence Newman's face is barely off the screen, and the close-ups are very tight indeed. This is partly to offer the simple pleasure of the star as spectacle, but it also has a narrative function of setting up expectations of toughness and the traditional western hero which are wryly overturned in the exchange with the guard. This will be no ordinary western.

A similar, if more elaborate, procedure occurs in the following scene. The film is still sepia, still a visual blending of myth and history. We move almost immediately to a close-up of the Sundance Kid/Robert Redford's face. He is playing cards at a table, facing the camera which shoots between two other players. These players are occasionally seen in silhouette, but the *mise-en-scène* ensures that the centre of interest is Sundance's face. The lighting is low-key, with most of the light coming from the right side, flaring out in Sundance's hair, but picking up skin textures, the texture of his thick corduroy jacket, and reflecting off one eye when it looks up at his opponents during the card game. Throughout the scene, Redford remains virtually expressionless but the spectacle of his face varies as he moves in and out of the light, and as his eyes move in and out of the shadows. In a direct parallel with the preceding sequence, his face is offered to the audience for its own sake, although the close-up is less tight, less dependent on an instant recognition of the star's features.

As the card game proceeds, the camera stays on Redford's face but we hear the preamble to, and eventually the delivery of, the charge of cheating against Sundance. Immediately, figures on either side of the screen move out of sight, we hear chairs scraping, and the scenario for the gunfight is set. The accuser stands up, facing Sundance across the table, although we only see past his gun hand as we watch for Sundance's reaction. The card-player dominates Sundance in the frame (Sundance has to look up at him), but he is at the extreme left of the frame, and his face has not yet been seen by the audience. The silence which now falls, and the stillness of Sundance's face, make it a moment of some tension and expectation.

Into this tense moment, comes Butch's incongruously cheerful voice: 'We seem to be short of brotherly love around here.' As Butch attempts to intercede, Sundance finally reveals some expression as he insists, childishly, 'I *wasn't* cheating.' Instead of proceeding immediately to the gunfight, the film enters into an affectionate parody of the conventions of the western genre. Butch remonstrates, telling Sundance not to fight, and moves into the frame behind Sundance's shoulder – talking into his ear like an irritating conscience. The camera still holds its close-up on Redford with Newman's face behind him and to one side. Redford is expressionless, even when Newman warns, '*I'm* over the hill, but it *can* happen to you.' The tactlessness of this suggestion just before a gunfight is comic, and the comedy is furthered when Butch starts on the card-player, suggesting a compromise. Sundance's pride has been wounded, and he says he won't leave until the card-player asks him to stay. The perverseness of this is underlined when Butch pleads: 'Just ask us to stick around – you don't even have to mean it!' Throughout his intercession with the card-player, the camera stays on Butch's face as it looks up ingenuously. When he is finally pushed away, Butch drops the guise of the genial fool, turns his classic profile, and tells Sundance

'I can't help you, Sundance.' An immediate cut to the face of the card-player (the first time we see his face) registers his disquiet at the name. This is followed by a medium long shot of the conventional gunfight tableau: the camera is behind the card-player, looking past his gun hand to Sundance who now stands up ready to draw. The tension is built up through a series of cuts between the worried card-player, the cajoling Butch ('go on, just say it') and the impassive Sundance. 'I didn't know you were the Sundance Kid,' says the card-player; 'if I draw on you, you'll kill me.' The tide has now turned, and the camera pulls back into the medium long shot of the tableau again as the card-player finally says 'Why don't you stick around?' Butch grins in an aw-shucks manner and says 'Thanks, we gotta get going', and the tension is dissipated, the moment made ridiculous by the silliness of the ritual just played out.

However, that is not the end of the sequence. The camera stays with its medium long shot and Butch moves in towards the table to sweep Sundance's winnings into his hat. Meanwhile Sundance walks past the card-player towards the camera on his way out. As he reaches the far left foreground of the screen, the card-player, who is behind him but central, calls, 'Hey, Kid, how good are you?' At this, the sequence explodes into action. Sundance drops into the classic gunfighter crouch, and fires his gun with a speed exaggerated by the quick intercutting of shots of the gun leaving its holster, the card-player's holster being shot from his hip, and his gun spinning across the floor as successive shots hit it. We see Sundance frontally at first, shooting straight at the camera; this magnifies the power of the action. He is then seen from the side, and finally through a close-up of the nonchalant twirl of his revolver as he replaces it in his holster. Throughout, Butch has continued to sweep up the money, and now he walks towards Sundance and the camera. The two move out together as Butch remarks, 'Like I been tellin' ya, over the hill.'

The sequence offers a complicated mixture of mythologizing and parody of the conventions of the western. Just when we see the confrontation averted through the parody of gunfight conventions, the power of the gunfighter is reinvoked, remythologized in the impossible series of shots Sundance is represented as executing. Clearly the film is going to define its own relation to the western genre, and it will be a complex and witty relationship. It is also clear from these sequences that the main characters will be able to have it both ways: they can be witty and self-deprecating, and thus not believe in their own mythologies; but they can also be powerful heroes possessing genuine skills, courage, and coolness. A heady mix, particularly when combined with two stars of the appeal of Newman and Redford.

These opening sequences are an introduction to the film, establishing the main characters and the visual and narrative style. The sequence immediately following depicts the two heroes riding across country to their Hole in the Wall hideout. By the end of this sequence the sepia tones have modulated and disappeared, the most self-conscious of the mythologizing has been done, and the narrative proper can begin. It is an economical and engaging opening, representative of the kind of wit that also informs George Roy Hill's second film with the same stars, *The Sting* (1973).

I have concentrated on the formal elements of the film text up to this point, making minimal references to the role of the audience in understanding this film. It is necessary to point out how actively the audience participates in the generation of the meanings of these two sequences. For a start, the offer of (at least) two viewing positions (one identifying with the nostalgic past and the other with the knowing present) gives the film a semiotic richness in the range of positions from which it can make sense. Further, the film invites the audience to recognize how self-conscious it is. There is a degree of complicity in the relationship between the film and its audience which establishes a nostalgic and affectionate point of view on the outlaws while still gently sending up the mythology of the western outlaw. The competencies of the audiences are also tested, even flattered, by the film; as they 'pass' the test they are rewarded with a deeper understanding of the film and of the processes of its construction. Not only is the audience asked to recognize the parodies of the western in order to find the opening sequences comic, but they are also offered the most cryptic of narratives: the card-game sequence depicts a series of actions involving several characters (playing cards, falling still at the challenge to Sundance, pushing their chairs back and leaving) whom we never actually see; we construct this narrative from aural clues alone as the camera stays fixed in close-up on Redford's face.

Again, although my intention here is to focus on the details of the text, it is important to suggest how one might extend the analysis to deal with the film's social and ideological dimensions. The giant close-ups of Newman and Redford in these sequences are excessive, exaggerated, overtly mythologizing. The result is parodic as well as myth-making. *Butch Cassidy and the Sundance Kid* is able to benefit from the spectacle of the star's face while also burlesquing and thus subverting the heroic individualism identified with conventional representations of the western hero. As Wright (1975) has pointed out, the romanticism and individualism of the classic western (which are implicated in the mythologizing close-up) are modified and eventually rejected in such 'professional' westerns as *Butch Cassidy and the Sundance Kid*. The power of the western hero is still exploited visually, but narratively and ideologically it is subverted. The specific sense of anachronism established in the opening sequences of *Butch Cassidy and the Sundance Kid* eventually applies to the western itself; its faith in individual power has little purchase in the film's version of an encroaching twentieth century. Nevertheless, while Butch and Sundance may be fallible and naïve, this does not make them less attractive or less interesting; although they have little narrative power (events happen *to* them), the close-ups ensure that they have enormous power as images.

When I discussed the western in Chapter 4, I referred to Metz's view (1982) that genres ultimately become critical of themselves; that is, films which are recognizably westerns nevertheless set out to attack the conventions and the supporting ideologies of their own genre. It is not difficult to see *Butch Cassidy and the Sundance Kid* in this way. It can self-consciously exploit our nostalgia for these heroic individuals *because* they have lost their relevance; the film imagines no place for them within contemporary ideological structures. Its sceptical evaluation of Butch and Sundance, and of all they stand for, is acted out in the final freeze frame of the pair facing death optimistically, quixotically, and finally. In *Butch Cassidy and the Sundance Kid* we can see just how the western has changed its meaning, and its relation to dominant ideological positions.

In the last few paragraphs I have moved away from the form of the film text to areas of interaction between the text and the audience, and ultimately the culture. It is important to be aware that meanings do not sit in the text waiting to be recognized – they are produced by the act of reading the film within a specific cultural context. However, from this brief account, it should be clear how the placement of elements within the frame, lighting, film stock, and the sound-track can contribute to the meaning of a film. This kind of analysis is necessary before any more general conclusions can be drawn, and yet it is also the most straightforward of practices. It simply requires that one be observant and relate what is seen and heard to functions within the narrative. It is, then, a starting-point. We can take a similar starting-point in the next analysis, but we will take it further – exploring other approaches outlined in earlier chapters.

DESPERATELY SEEKING SUSAN

In Chapter 4 I listed the following oppositions as those which structure the narrative in *Desperately Seeking Susan*:

Roberta	Susan
conventional	unconventional
bourgeois	anti-bourgeois
suburban	urban
married	unmarried
sexually submissive	sexually aggressive
boring	exciting
constrained	free

I pointed out that these structures shape more than the 'plot'; they also determine the ways in which this plot will be represented. So, although this set of oppositions was enclosed within an analysis of the narrative structure, it could as easily have emerged from a close analysis of the representational motifs of the *mise-en-scène*. For example, an account of the *mise-en-scène* at the beginning of the film would make some of the following points.

In the opening sequences, *Desperately Seeking Susan* regularly cuts back and forth between Roberta and Susan in order to introduce the elements of the plot – the stolen ear-rings, the villain, the central characters. However, the cross-cutting both pairs and juxtaposes Susan and Roberta by comparing and contrasting their lifestyles, their reactions to similar stimuli, and their cultural or subcultural contexts.

The first sequence takes place in a beauty salon, an assembly line of women having manicures or 'beauty treatments', or having their hair styled. Roberta is situated within this world through the framing, the pink tones of the salon's décor and the women's protective smocks, and (ideologically) by her plea to the hairdresser not to do anything 'weird' to her hair. The image of constrained femininity is capped in the following sequence which has Roberta and her sister-in-law framed under the hairdryers – a parody of middle-class suburbia. However, it is in this sequence that we gain our first hint of some resistance in Roberta. She notes the advertisement in the Personals column which is headed 'Desperately Seeking Susan', and reveals that she has been following its story for some time. Her romantic enthusiasm for the word 'desperate' suggests she is ripe for an adventure. After she circles the advertisement we cut to a new location and subject. An establishing shot of an Atlantic City hotel is followed by a slow tracking shot, back from the pink scalloped curtains in Susan's hotel room to Susan herself – lying on the floor taking pictures of herself with a polaroid camera. The pink in the curtains may remind us of Roberta's social world, but in most other respects we are conscious of a radical difference. The room is full of signifiers of pleasure and excess. Susan's clothes are bizarre in design, black in colour, and anything but suburban in their effect. The rich disorder of the room is the antithesis of the a-septic machine-room business of the hairdressing salon.

Despite these contrasts, a link between Roberta and Susan is established as the next move in the plot is made. We find out that Susan is the girl addressed in the advertisement when she recognizes it, and draws a flamboyant heart around it with her eyeliner. She then steals money and the Egyptian ear-rings from her sleeping mate, packs her things, and leaves by the lift – under the gaze of the villain. When we return to Roberta's world it is through a brief establishing shot of her house, followed by a cut to its interior where her birthday party is in progress. Signifiers of boring suburbia abound. The plate of hors-d'œuvres fills the screen, Carly Simon is on the stereo, and one woman is wearing the same dress as Roberta. When her husband Gary calls a halt to the proceedings in order to watch a TV advertisement for his bathroom spa business, we understand the full limits of Roberta's domestic horizon. As the ad plays to the party audience, Roberta walks to the window. The camera follows her out on to the balcony, where she looks at the bridge linking New Jersey to New York. In the background we hear the last line of the spa advertisement: 'Come to Gary's Oasis, where all your fantasies can come true.' We are offered a subjective shot of the magically lit bridge; it is the division between the two worlds and thus an image of escape, or 'desperation' for Roberta. As Roberta looks at it, the music track goes up tempo and we cut to a bus arriving in New York City carrying Susan and the ear-rings. Soon, Roberta will drive across that bridge to observe Susan meet her 'desperate' suitor, Jim, and the plot will take off.

This alternating narrative movement establishes what Susan, Roberta, and their respective worlds might be like and what they might mean, by carefully depicting those worlds. All the systems of signification work to construct a network of difference and similarity between the contexts and the characters. An important component, for instance, is the music track. In the opening sequence in the beauty salon we listen to a 1960s 'girly' group, an emblem of old-fashioned romanticism and, less obviously, male domination. When we move to Susan's world it is rock and roll of a more contemporary, unromantic, and insistent kind – the song is 'Urgent'. We could follow the parts played by the various systems of signification further, but my essential point here is to establish the connections between the narrative structure and the languages used to represent it.

The preceding discussion of *Butch Cassidy* concluded with the introduction of an ideological reading. We can explore this approach further here. The position that *Desperately Seeking Susan* appears to take towards conventional gender roles (the wife as suburban home-maker, for instance) invites one to see it as a film which foregrounds its social and ideological dimensions.

The ideological invitation into *Desperately Seeking Susan* is sent by the fact that the oppositions described earlier set up a film where Roberta's quest is not so much for a Mr Right as for a member of her own sex who can provide a corrective and progress-ive role model. Although Roberta finally dumps Gary in favour of the more appealing and less suburban Dez, the audience is by no means certain to see that as the key action of the film. The patterning of oppositions and linkages between Roberta and Susan (the way in which Roberta 'becomes' Susan for Dez, the villain, and for the viewer in her adoption of Susan's jacket, hairstyle, and ultimately name) generates a tension that is only resolved when the two women meet. Although it is not, like *Outrageous Fortune*, a female 'buddy' movie, the relations between the women are crucial to the film.

There is a feminist set of ideologies at work in *Desperately Seeking Susan* which enables Susan to be the most powerful and self-possessed of the characters and has the men stand by and

watch rather than influence the plot's development. Even when
the villain is caught it is Roberta who knocks him out with a bottle.
The following scene, in which Roberta and Susan recognize each
other, has the structural importance of the lovers' first kiss in a
conventional romantic comedy. It resolves and repairs the tensions
generated by the rest of the film. But it is understated. Audiences
have expressed their disappointment at the lack of a stronger sense
of recognition or, even, destiny at this moment. The film seems to
deflect the expectations from this meeting by immediately taking
us to a more conventional romantic reunion between Roberta and
Dez in the projection room of the theatre. This is the second in a
series of points of closure to the narrative. It is followed by a third
point: a shot of Susan and her boyfriend Jim in the cinema, eating
popcorn and enjoying each other's company. The foursome which
this establishes would not be out of place in the most conventional
romantic comedy. Yet this is followed by still another conclud-
ing sequence of newspaper pages announcing the return of the
Egyptian ear-rings, a reward for Susan and Roberta, and a cele-
bratory civic reception. The headline 'What a Pair!' is above a
photograph of Susan and Roberta, without Jim and Dez, holding
their hands aloft in a victory gesture. In this series of closing
sequences we are offered two possibly opposite kinds of closure in
that we are asked to celebrate two kinds of 'pairs' – the romantic
couple, and 'sisters'.

Why this should matter to the audience is that it raises the
possibility that the feminist stance of the film, the concentration
on the female protagonists and the depiction of the males as
peripheral to the plot, is blurred and defeated by the invoca-
tions of conventional romance. Admittedly, the scenes are
themselves comic and self-conscious and thus distance themselves from the conventional. However, the repeated moves
towards closure are markers of uncertainty, of the width of the
ideological gap which has been opened in the film, and which
now must be sealed over.

The specific function of the casting of Madonna is worth ques-
tioning, too. Although the film is, in a sense, a 'women's film', the
ideology of femaleness it constructs is complicated by Madonna.
On the one hand, her characterization of Susan represents her as
cool, capable, independent, and sexually manipulative – all conventionally masculine attributes. On the other hand, Madonna
herself has been offered as a commodity to her male and female

fans through the Boy Toy tag which undercuts progressive notions of the female.

I am aware that Madonna can be seen as a figure who exaggerates (and therefore makes ridiculous) male expectations of female sexuality; she therefore has a potentially feminist meaning. John Fiske (1987a) has examined the 'bundle of meanings' we think of as Madonna and argued that despite her apparent reproduction of a masculine view of women as objects of desire, the way in which she represents herself can be seen as critical and subversive of such masculine points of view. Drawing on interviews with fans as well as textual analysis of her music videos, Fiske claims Madonna's 'knowing' use of the camera enables her to mock 'the conventional representations of female sexuality at the same time she conforms to them':

> Madonna consistently parodies conventional representations of women and parody can be an effective device for interrogating the dominant ideology. It takes the defining features of its object, exaggerates and mocks them, and thus mocks those who 'fall' for its ideological effect. But Madonna's parody goes further than this; she parodies, not just the stereotypes, but the way in which they are made.
>
> (1987a: 277)

It is this aspect of her representation of herself, her control of her image rather than her subjection to it, which seems to strike a chord in her fans. Fiske quotes one fan who can see that the 'tarty and seductive' looks are potentially sexist, but nevertheless feels that 'it's OK with her'. Madonna is seen as the producer of her image, not merely its bearer; that changes the meaning of the image. Paradoxically, the sense of Madonna's personal and sexual independence seems to derive from her explicit appropriation of images of female sexuality; with Madonna, gestures of submission can be double-edged and work as a challenge to the sexuality of the masculine observer. The excessiveness of Madonna's depiction of female sexuality is its most parodic and intimidating aspect and in it we can see a wealth of meanings other than the simple Boy Toy label; or rather, the label itself becomes ironic, a flippant taunt to the masculine. Who is likely to 'toy' with whom? is the question posed by the image of Madonna.

Fiske's account of the meanings attributable to Madonna would lead us to see her casting as entirely consonant with the film's meanings. Nevertheless, for viewers who do not see Madonna in such a way, her casting must have set up awkward ideological contradictions.

It is worth stressing here that what I have been offering are suggestions towards readings, not any kind of definitive account. Each approach outlined in this book has the potential to produce a different account of the film – in effect, a different film. In my suggestions I have incorporated information made available by the semiotics of stars, by structuralist accounts of narrative, by *mise-en-scène* criticism, and by ideological theory. The virtue of exploring a number of approaches lies in the fact that the different versions can complement, mirror, or challenge each other. The result is a sense of the complexity of the communication which is occurring, of the film's potential for meaning, as well as of the suspect nature of any claim to definitive or final readings. The ideological argument just mounted, for instance, depends on a number of unexamined assumptions. One is that *Desperately Seeking Susan* is a 'women's film' – itself a category which bears closer interrogation. To see *Desperately Seeking Susan* in this way is to place it in a particular genre, and that demands some argument.

If we consider *Desperately Seeking Susan* through notions of genre we immediately recover a sense of its playfulness and assurance, features that are subordinated in the ideological reading. *Desperately Seeking Susan* plays conflicting generic expectations off against each other, moving from one set of conventions to another with a degree of skill and self-awareness. It may start out as a film which foregrounds the opposition constructed between the worlds and thus the ideologies of its main characters, but it quickly tells us that the rules which the narrative will follow are those of genre, not the 'real world'. Roberta's subjection is exaggerated and made comic; her birthday closes with her sitting with the remains of her cake watching a rerun of the archetypal romantic weepie, *Rebecca*, on the TV. The opposition between her life and Susan's is too stark to require interpretation; rather, it becomes the structural basis for the film's narrative. Similarly, when we follow Susan leaving her hotel room, she spills her belongings on the floor in front of the lift. The lift has just discharged a passenger who looks at Susan for an exceptionally long time, and then slowly walks off, shoes squeaking theatrically. We have just met the villain, and the character's general – if not specific –

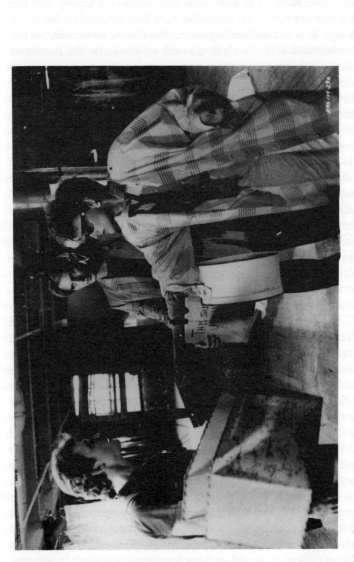

19 Dez (Aidan Quinn) separates from his 'ex' (Anna Carlisle) in *Desperately Seeking Susan* (used with permission, courtesy of Village Roadshow)

audience whose main objective would be to see a 'Madonna' film. The placement of *Desperately Seeking Susan* within the genre of teen movies would be of some commercial benefit, since this is the largest sector of the cinema market. However, it does seem clear that most audiences who were encouraged to see the film as a teen movie or a Madonna film were disappointed. While the film deals with a similar set of conflicts to *Risky Business, The Breakfast Club*, and other teen movies – conflicts between individual self-expression, say, and social restraints – they are articulated in different ways. In the teen movies, the key constraining influences are parents and school. The hero's or heroine's articulation of independence, or pursuit of pleasure, occurs in spite of and against the ideologies and prohibitions of their family, teachers, or adult advisers. *Desperately Seeking Susan* takes the battle a stage beyond this, to the choice of marriage, examining less specific social pressures towards conformity and compromise. So while one could expect the audience for John Hughes's movies to sympathise with Roberta's plight, they are not likely to identify in the same way that they do with the main character in *Risky Business*. *Desperately Seeking Susan* is a film about the difficulties of adulthood and definitions of femininity.

We see films within specific social conditions, and take to them our own set of views of the world. Any reading of a film is only that, one reading. To approach *Desperately Seeking Susan* from one set of assumptions as to what kind of film it is may produce a different film to that perceived by another viewer with a different set of assumptions. There are limits to this process, of course, but the argument about a film's genre is ultimately an argument about what it *is*; it is not surprising that those who disagree on what kind of film they are watching will also disagree on specific details. But divergent or competing readings are not necessarily contradictory of each other. *Desperately Seeking Susan* is, in a sense, many kinds of film. It consciously takes exhilarating risks in order to keep options open, to provide a multiplicity of positions from which it can provide its audiences with the pleasures of cinema. To attempt to reduce that multiplicity to one unitary point of view would be to lose much; also, it would lose sight of the point of this exercise, which is to explore different approaches for their ability to produce a different text. This potential is a benefit, not a threat, to anyone attempting to understand popular cinema and its relations to its audiences.

Thompson, K. (1985) *Exporting Entertainment: America in the World Film Market 1907–1934*, London: British Film Institute.

Todorov, T. (1977) *The Poetics of Prose*, Oxford: Blackwell.

Tudor, A. (1974) *Image and Influence*, London: Allen & Unwin.

Tulloch, J. (1982) *Australian Cinema: Industry, Narrative and Meaning*, Sydney: Allen & Unwin.

Turner, G. (1986) *National Fictions: Literature, Film and the Construction of Australian Narrative*, Sydney: Allen & Unwin.

Williamson, D. (1986) *Authorship and Criticism*, Sydney: Local Consumption.

Williamson, J. (1987) *Consuming Passions*, London: Marion Boyars.

Wollen, P. (1972) *Signs and Meanings in the Cinema*, London: Secker & Warburg.

—— (1976) 'North by North-West: a morphological analysis', *Film Form* 1 (2).

Wright, W. (1975) *Six Guns and Society: a Structural Study of the Western*, Berkeley: University of California Press.

Index